D1478951

In this very readable (and yes, engaging) book, John Guaspari reminds us that great leaders create an environment which connects people to what is important for them as well as the company. Using a simple metaphor and providing clear, specific actions which a new or experienced leader can take, Guaspari shows us that, in the PowerPoint world of analysis and logic that permeates most organizations, it is really our humanity, and feelings of trust, respect, and safety that generate commitment and therefore performance. Pick up this book. You will learn that a wise leader doesn't try to motivate people but rather understands "the intangibles" that motivate us all.

— **David Dotlich, Ph.D.**
  Chairman and CEO, Pivot Leadership
  Author of *The Unfinished Leader* and 10 other leadership books

Otherwise Engaged is vintage Guaspari: clever and entertaining while also substantive, thought provoking, and wise.

— **Dan Ciampa**
  Coauthor of *Right From The Start: Taking Charge In A New Leadership Role*

An engagingly funny fable that John Guaspari uses to guide the reader to answer the profoundly serious question posed by the book – Why do employee engagement activities often fail? … Thought-provoking and charming.

— **Jim Kouzes**
  Dean's Executive Fellow of Leadership, Leavey School of Business, Santa Clara University, and coauthor of the bestselling book, T*he Leadership Challenge.*

Having worked with John Guaspari in a previous life, I can unequivocally say that he practices what he preaches. Anyone in a position of leadership at any level would be well advised to take the advice John provides in *Otherwise Engaged*.

— **Gen. James B. Smith**
   Former U.S. Ambassador to Saudi Arabia

Employee engagement has been the elusive holy grail for companies and leadership since surveys revealed there is a serious gap between what we believe creates engagement and reality. This is a story that has been ongoing with no conclusion. Guaspari tells the story that needed telling, and he does it using humor and metaphor like only he can. This is a fun book that packs a powerful message all business leaders must hear to finally engage their people.

— **David Casullo**
   President, Bates Communications
   Author of *Leading the High Energy Culture: What the Best CEOs Do to Create an Atmosphere Where Employees Flourish*

John Guaspari's latest book *Otherwise Engaged* is a must-read in today's highly packaged, productized, and transactional business environment. It reminds anyone who aspires to fully lead others that they must genuinely unleash (rather than pay lip service to) the vital intangibles of engagement and respect.

— **Paul Allen**
   Chairman, Allen & Gerritsen
   Multiple Awardee: "One of the Best Places to Work in Boston"

An insightful and fresh perspective on contemporary talent and organizational effectiveness topics – engagement, empowerment, values, trust – in a useful and practical narrative … it will challenge you to think differently as you implement solutions to human capital issues.

— **Joe Bonito**
    Senior Vice President, Ledership Development Executive,
    Global Human Resources, Bank of America

John Guaspari takes the vagaries of intangibles and serves up a hilarious how-to with his latest avatars, the Wilson family. *Otherwise Engaged* provides a solid approach to the elusive topic of employee engagement. Guaspari's brilliance is his airtight logic, but lucky for us each "aha!" is paired with a "ha ha!" – a business book rarity. I'll take it!

— **Elisabeth Swan**
    President, Swan Consulting & Associates, Inc.

Otherwise Engaged should be required reading for anyone in a leadership position in any type of organization. You'll come away understanding how critically important employee engagement is to the achievement of personal and business objectives. And John Guaspari's writing style and wit make it an easy and enjoyable read.

— **Walter J. Flaherty**
    COO and CFO, New England Aquarium (Ret.)

Otherwise Engaged

Otherwise Engaged

How Leaders Can
Get a Firmer Grip on
Employee Engagement and
Other Key Intangibles*

* If, That Is, It Were Possible to Grip
Something That's Intangible

John Guaspari

MAVEN HOUSE
PRESS

Published by Maven House Press, 4 Snead Ct., Palmyra, VA 22963; 610.883.7988; www.mavenhousepress.com.

Special discounts on bulk quantities of Maven House Press books are available to corporations, professional associations, and other organizations. For details contact the publisher.

Illustrations by Maria Lucia Cortina

While this publication is designed to provide accurate and authoritative information in regard to the subject matter covered, it is sold with the understanding that the publisher is not engaged in rendering legal, accounting, or other professional service. If legal advice or other expert assistance is required, the services of a competent professional person should be sought. – From the Declaration of Principles jointly adopted by a Committee of the American Bar Association and a Committee of Publishers and Associations

Library of Congress Control Number: 2014957206

Hardcover ISBN: 978-1-938548-33-8
ePUB ISBN: 978-1-938548-34-5
ePDF ISBN: 978-1-938548-35-2

Printed in the United States of America.

10 9 8 7 6 5 4 3 2 1

DEDICATION

For Daniel Rej,
a young man who gets it

CONTENTS

FOREWORD

by Jim Kouzes

L EADERSHIP IS A RELATIONSHIP. It's a relationship between those
who aspire to lead and those who choose to follow. It's the *qual-ity* of this relationship that matters most when making extraordinary
things happen. A leader-constituent relationship that's characterized
by fear and distrust will never produce anything of lasting value. A
relationship characterized by mutual respect and trust will overcome
the greatest adversities and leave a legacy of significance. This is the
larger lesson that Matt and Jennifer Wilson struggle to get across
in this engagingly funny fable that John Guaspari uses to guide the
reader to answer the profoundly serious question posed by the book
– why do employee engagement activities often fail.

The Wilsons teach us that success in leadership, in work, and in
life has been, is now, and will always be a function of how well people work and play together. Success is wholly dependent upon the
capacity to build and sustain human relationships. Because leadership is a reciprocal process between leaders and their constituents,
any discussion of leadership must attend to the dynamics of this relationship. Strategies, tactics, skills, and all the clever consulting techniques — like the ones the Wilsons apply in their family improvement
project — are empty without an understanding of the fundamental
human aspirations that connect leaders and constituents.

But there's another and more subtle message in this tale of *Oth-erwise Engaged*. It's a lesson we learn early but seem to forget. It's a
lesson about who the true leaders really are.

For over thirty years my coauthor, Barry Posner, and I have been asking people to tell us who their leader role models are. Not well-known historical leaders, but leaders with whom they've had personal experience. We've given them a list of eight possible categories from which these leaders might come. They can choose from business leader, community or religious leader, entertainer or cinema star, family member, political leader, professional athlete, teacher or coach, or other/none/not sure.

We have found consistently over time that regardless of age, when thinking back and selecting their most important leader role models, people are more likely to choose a family member than anyone else. It turns out that mom and dad, grandma and grandpa, sister and brother, and aunt and uncle are the most influential leaders in our lives. In second place for respondents thirty years of age and under are teachers or coaches. For the over thirty group business leaders are number two. When we probe further, people tell us that the business leader they were thinking about was an immediate supervisor at work, not someone in the C-suite; for those in the workplace these leaders are their teachers and coaches.

Notice what the top two leader role model categories have in common. They are the leaders we are closest to and who are closest to us. They're the ones with whom we have the most intimate contact. They're the ones we know best and who know us best. Leader role models are local.

That means to some people *you* could be their leader role model. You don't have to look up for leadership. You don't have to look out for leadership. You only have to look inward. *You* have the potential to lead others to places they have never been before. And if you are someone's role model of leadership, then don't you have the responsibility to be the best role model you can be?

But keep in mind that leadership is not about the leader. It is *not* about *you*. It is about others. It is about how others experience you and what you do. It's about *their* hopes, dreams, and aspirations. It's about *their* level of trust, respect, and engagement with you and each other. It's about *their* feelings of empowerment and commitment.

A while back when my wife and I were in Truckee, California, a small town in the Sierra Mountains near Lake Tahoe, we stopped at a shop that was once a railway station. As we walked up the wooden steps to the building, we noticed a carved wooden sign affixed to the exterior clapboard wall. The sign read: "This building is dedicated to the memory of Ignatius Joseph Firpo. 'What we have done for ourselves dies with us; What we have done for others remains and is immortal.'" Ignatius Joseph Firpo, to his friends, family, and coworkers, was clearly someone who made others the center of his world.

And that is really the point of this thought-provoking and charming book you are about to read. Enjoy.

* * *

Jim Kouzes is the coauthor of the bestselling book, *The Leadership Challenge,* and the Dean's Executive Fellow of Leadership, Leavey School of Business, Santa Clara University.

INTRODUCTION

"Leadership is the art of getting someone else to do
what you want done because he wants to do it."

— *President Dwight D. Eisenhower*

THIS BOOK IS ABOUT LEADERSHIP, the defining characteristic of
which is the existence of followers. For our purposes, *leader* can
mean a C-level executive or it can mean a frontline supervisor. It
can mean a person with explicit positional authority over a business
unit of a Fortune 100 company as well as someone called on to head
up an eight-person, ad hoc project team who must lead through
influence alone.

It's also about Engagement, a concept that's popping up more and
more often on leaders' screens these days. And that's for a very good
reason. Compelling research done by CEB, Gallup, Hay Group, and
others demonstrates the indisputable correlation between high levels of Employee Engagement and substantially improved business
results, as measured along such critical dimensions as profitability,
productivity, and employee retention rates.

Engagement doesn't happen in a vacuum, though. Focusing on
it inevitably means coming face-to-face with such related matters as
Empowerment, Trust, Respect, Company Values, and the rest of the
so-called soft stuff… the people stuff.

Attending to all of this effectively is a non-trivial challenge. But
leaders don't become leaders by backing down when faced with such

challenges. They take action – the *summum bonum* of complex organizational life – by launching serious-minded, well-funded initiatives to drive up Engagement levels, appropriately genuflecting along the way to Engagement's first cousins, the other Intangibles. They do their homework, researching the currently accepted tools and techniques, settling not just for any practices, but only for *best* practices.

It's all very sensible, logical, and rational, and often as not, the results come up short of expectations. So the question becomes: Why?

It's a question I've been trying to help leaders in hundreds of organizations representing scores of industries answer for thirty-plus years now.* Over all that time, there have been two incidents that, more than any others, brightly illuminated just what the answer might be. Here's one of them.

I was standing on the stage of a corporate auditorium. The title of the presentation I was about to make was the standard one I used in such instances: "Making the Business Case for *The Intangibles*." If you were to try to imagine a group of people predisposed to be skeptical about this sort of subject matter, you'd be hard pressed to come up with a better one than the hundred or so people I was facing at that moment: the security team of a business unit of a major technology company. Suffice it to say, these are not people whose day-planners tend to be overfilled with matters pertaining to the soft stuff.

A few days earlier I had told a colleague that this assignment would be a piece of cake: "All I have to do is make a logical, left-brained argument to an overwhelmingly logical, left-brained audience that logical, left-brained arguments aren't enough." I was joking, but I also knew that this pretty well captured the essence of the challenge before me. I believed that what I had to say had the potential to be of considerable value, even to such logical, left-brained folks. That wouldn't be the case, though, unless I could find a way to get past the Starship Enterprise-grade deflector shields that such audiences reflexively deploy – set to eleven – when under threat of bombardment by what they perceived to be such Kumbaya-ish subject matter.

---

* It wasn't called Engagement back then. In retrospect, though, it becomes clear that that's what it was.

So I took a risk. Instead of beginning my presentation by talking *about* the Intangibles, I decided to try to get them to vicariously *feel* one.

I began by telling them the story of what had happened on the evening our son Mike was born some thirty years earlier. I described my wife Gail announcing that the big moment had arrived, the phone calls to the hospital and obstetrician, the gathering up of the go-bags, the short/long three-mile drive to the hospital. I told them of how the song that happened to be playing on the car radio when I turned the ignition key was Billy Joel's "Piano Man," and that by the end of the song we had arrived at the hospital, that by the end of the night mother and baby were doing great.

Here's how I concluded the story: "To this day, whenever I hear 'Piano Man,' I get a powerful emotional jolt. I cannot prove it to you. I cannot show it to you. I cannot put it in front of you so that you can touch it, or taste it, or smell it. But don't you *dare* try to tell me that this feeling is not real. What's more, everyone in this room has an equivalent story to tell about something that will trigger a deeply rooted bit of sense memory and give you that same kind of emotional jolt. That's what I mean by *The Intangibles.* That's what we're going to be talking about for the next hour or so."

It worked. I could tell by the body language that their deflector shields had come down. Most of all, I could tell when, at the end of the hour, I thanked them for their time and attention and exited stage left, at which point one of those oh-so-logical/rational security professionals held up his iPhone – volume cranked up to eleven – and serenaded us all with Billy Joel's "Piano Man."

That was one of the most gratifying moments of my professional career. What happened next, however, was not.

A fifteen-minute break was called, and an HR director for the business unit approached me.

"May I offer you some constructive feedback?" she asked.

"Of course!" I replied.

"This is a pretty diverse group," she said. "Not all of them are baby boomers like you and I are. So their tastes in music are likely to be different from ours. I think your story would have been more effective if instead of using a song by Billy Joel you had used one by someone like, say, Katy Perry."

What I said in reply was this: "Hmm. Interesting point. I'll be sure to give it some thought."

What I had wanted to say was this: "But that's what actually, you know, *happened*. 'Piano Man' is the song that was on the radio! An hour ago I stood up in front of these people and opened a vein and shared a deeply personal, deeply emotional story!! One that I had never shared in public before!!! I understand that this is a diverse team and that, Lord knows, they're all the stronger as a result!!!! But 'Piano Man' is what was on the radio that night!!!!! *And besides which, Katy Perry is younger than Mike!!!!!*"

All of which goes to prove yet again that attempting to deal with the Intangibles is like trying to lasso a cloud. Don't get me wrong. I am more than prepared to concede that she may have missed the point of the "Piano Man" story because of my shortcomings as a presenter. But the guy who held up the iPhone seemed to get it. So, too, did all of the people who sang along to "Piano Man" when he did. So how was it that an HR director – *an HR director!* – didn't?

I think it has to do with the fact that leaders have a strong bias toward logical, rational, data-driven solutions to problems. It's a bias that is reinforced by the dynamic push and pull of organizational life. You don't become a leader – or at least you won't be a leader for long – by relying on gut feelings and emotion alone.

For the record, I am not immune to the appeal of such a worldview. Both my undergraduate and graduate training were in aerospace engineering, and I spent the first several years of my career in that profession. I, too, like to be data-driven.

But doesn't the fact that so many well-intentioned initiatives fall short of expectations represent important data? In what sense are you being data-driven when you come up short and think, "We did our best. But, you know, it's the soft stuff that's the hard part, so ...," thereby shrugging away the possibility that maybe the approach that was taken wasn't so sensible and rational after all?

Which brings us to the root of the problem, and I think it has to do with the fact that security professionals are not the only ones with hair-triggers on their deflector shields. Sad to say, pretty much everybody has them. It's just human nature.

Well-intentioned and sensible though they may be, those rational, well-resourced, best-practice-driven initiatives amount to the application of mechanical, utilitarian prescriptions to what is essentially a problem of the spirit and soul. It's not just that such approaches *don't* work. It's that they *can't* work, any more than even the most powerful antibiotic will cure a viral infection.

That's a costly problem for businesses, since they invest a lot in what has come to be called their human capital, and there are enormous benefits to be realized by leaders who are able to get a firmer grip on Engagement and all of its cousins – if, that is, it were possible to get a handle on those Intangibles, which by definition can't be touched.

A paradox that, and it's what we'll be covering over the next 138 pages. Such is the ambiguity of the leader's challenge. Embrace it. You might just as well, since you can't embrace the Intangibles themselves.

* * *

A few words about what you are about to read in "Part One: Getting a Firmer Grip on The Problem."

In it, you'll meet the Wilsons: the father, Matt; the mother, Jennifer; and their children, Matt Jr. and Jessica. You will be given a behind-the-scenes look at what happens when Matt (a high-powered management consultant) and Jen (a small-business owner) strategize about how they can best apply familiar business practices in their household so that: (1) their kids are fully engaged members of the Wilson clan; and (2) they, Matt and Jen, are more effective when it comes to attending to other key family Intangibles, such as Empowerment, Trust, Respect, and Values.

Obviously (or at least I hope it will be obvious), the Wilsons' story is a parable. No parents would ever take such an instrumental, mechanical approach to something as personal and sublime as their relationship with their children.

So why tell their story at all? Because – no surprise here – dealing effectively with the Intangibles is difficult to do well; if it weren't, you wouldn't be reading this book. And one of the things that makes it such a difficult challenge is the breathtaking complexity of modern organizational life. However committed we might be to getting a firmer "grip" on the intangibles,* the fact is that we've got a thousand-and-one-things pulling us in this-or-that direction, so our efforts might not be as focused as we would like them to be. And however well-intentioned we might be when making those efforts, some of the things we might wind up doing could actually, sad to say, do harm.

By observing what goes on in such a simple "organization" – four people, all co-located, all in frequent and direct contact with each other – we are better situated to isolate and discover the causal connection between the seemingly sensible techniques employed and the less-than-ideal results attained.

And who knows? You might even feel a pang or two of recognition along the way that makes you think: *That sounds uncomfortably familiar.* Maybe even: *Holy crap! I've been as big a knucklehead as Matt Wilson!*

The hope here, too, is that you will find the Wilsons' story entertaining and amusing enough to draw you through some of the abstract argumentation needed to help you get that firmer "grip" on those intangibles.

On to Part One.

---

* The quotation marks around "grip" absolve me from the need to add "if it were possible to get a grip on something that's intangible."

Getting a Firmer Grip on the Problem

CHAPTER 1

Meet the Wilsons

B Y ALL OUTWARD APPEARANCES, the Wilsons were the perfect family.

Matt was a high-powered, high-priced management consultant, dispensing advice to major corporate clients on important HR-related matters. (He had a sure-fire closing line for prospective clients: "If you really believe your people are your most valuable asset, then you won't choke when I tell you my fee!")

Jen was a successful owner and operator of a small business, "Jen's Jonquils 'n Stuff!" The name for the shop had been Matt's idea. Jen had initially been skeptical: "That 'n-Stuff part is a little cutesy for my blood." But Matt was used to dealing with skeptical clients, and he had skillfully persisted until he had secured Jen's buy-in. Then again, reasonable people could have interpreted her closing comment on the matter as less a matter of buying-in than of having been worn down: "Yeah. Fine. Whatever."

Happily married for nineteen years, the Wilsons could have filled up pages with lists of their accomplishments. But if you had asked them for such a list, it would have come back with just two items on it: their kids, Matt Jr. and Jessica.

Matt Jr. – everybody called him Skipper – was sixteen. An honor student and alto/baritone* in the church choir, Skipper was also a top-notch athlete, starting at quarterback on his school's football team, playing shortstop and batting clean-up on the baseball team, and following in Matt Sr.'s footsteps by holding down the anchor position on the Division IV Sectional Champion bowling team.

Jessica – Jess – was eleven. Even at such a young age, she was already on Skipper's heels in the gold-star department. Also an honor student, Jess was president of her middle school class. ("Jess is Besst!" had been her campaign slogan. Yes, Matt had helped out there, too.) And her dance instructor invariably put her in the front row for all of her numbers during the annual spring recital. Matt and Jen were always so excited to see Jess on stage, front and center, that they barely noticed that the cumulative time of her numbers – ten minutes – totaled less than five percent of the program's four-hour duration. (Skipper always noticed, but his sister had been a good sport about sitting in the bleachers for all of his games and bowling matches, so ...)

Following dinner on this particular night, after the kids had headed up to their rooms to tackle their homework, Matt returned to the kitchen table with a thick three-ring binder and several manila folders.

"What do you have there?" Jen asked.

"The results for the latest F-MOS," Matt said.

The first thought that this prompted in Jen's mind was *Good Lord, Matty ... no!* But you don't stay happily married for nineteen years by always blurting out the first thought that comes to mind. So Jen took a beat, composed herself, and said, "Ah. The results for the latest F-MOS. And what, pray tell, are they telling us?"

---

* A sixteen-year-old boy's voice is prone to sudden register changes.

4

This is probably a good time to point out that Matt had a pronounced tendency to conflate what may have been considered best practices on the job with best practices on the home front.

There was the time that he had rented the meeting room at the local Holiday Inn to serve as the site for the First Annual Wilson Family Quality/Six-Sigma Day! The kids, who were six and eleven at the time, thought that it was pretty neat to wear name tags and drink bottled water and what they called "fake coffee" – it was decaf – as they participated in what had been described on the day's pre-printed agenda as the Networking and Sharing Session. (They had been puzzled, though, by the If-you-were-a-tree-what-kind-would-you-be? ice-breaker.) For her part, Jen had fastened on the portentous implications of the word *Annual* in the event's name, making a solemn and ultimately successful vow to herself that *First* in this case would also mean *Last*.

Or the time that Matt did what he called a Value-Added Flow Analysis of the family's table-clearing-and-dishwasher-loading process as part of a Wilson Household Cycle-Time Reduction Initiative. The effort came up short of Matt's goal of reducing cycle time by 30 percent when Jen had refused to be part of the bucket-brigade-style line running from the kitchen table to the dishwasher. But it *had* revealed the need for a kanban system to eliminate instances when they would find themselves with a dishwasher full of dirty dishes but no detergent to clean them. ("Wasn't that discovery serendipitous?" Matt had asked. "I can think of a lot of adjectives to describe all of this," Jen had replied at the time, "but *serendipitous* ain't one of them.")

And who could forget the time that Matt decided to prove once and for all that there was a discernible difference between Coke and Diet Coke by running a taste test – double-blind, of course – during Jess's fourth birthday party. Matt was delighted that the results had supported his hypothesis. The parents of the 50 percent of the party's attendees who had been heavily-sugared as part of Matt's quest for knowledge were significantly less delighted, though, as they peeled their amped-up four-year-olds off the walls of the Wilsons' kitchen before managing to coax them into their cars for the drive home.

So, yes, Matt could be a bit quirky. But he was a good man and a devoted father and husband, so in the interest of marital comity, Jen had taken a beat, composed herself, and asked him about the results of the latest F-MOS – the Wilsons' Family-Member Opinion Survey.

"The results don't make any sense," Matt replied.

"How so?" Jen asked.

"We've been doing the F-MOS for five years now, and every year the results are the same," Matt said. "The scores have always been good for the more tangible things." He scanned the margin of his three-ring binder until he found the tabs he was looking for: "Quality of Housing Facilities, Square Footage of

Personal Space, Selection of Cable Channels, Vehicular Options, Sufficiency of Unstructured Hours, Food: Quality/Selection/ Availability, Medical Care, Recreational Equipment. All rated Excellent! And that's every year for five years!"

"So what's wrong with that?" Jen asked.

"Nothing! But it's when we get to the other stuff..." He riffled ahead to another tab – Intangibles. "...when we get to the Intangibles, that the scores are consistently lower. Values... Engagement... Empowerment...Trust & Respect. Those sorts of things."

"But haven't you always told me that those things are always the things that are trickiest for your clients?" Jen said. "What's that expression you always use...something about those things being the difficult part?"

"The expression is: 'It's the soft stuff that's the hard part,'" Matt replied. "And that's true. But it isn't as though we haven't been doing anything about those things. Remember when we decided to focus on Respect?"

Jen shrugged an I've-got-nothing shrug.

"It was three years ago," Matt said. "We tried some new things to improve our Respect scores, but it didn't seem to work. Did we stop there?"

Jen correctly assumed that this was a rhetorical question.

"No, we did not!" Matt continued, without so much as a pause. "We redoubled our efforts and launched a new-and-improved Respect program the following year. Do you remember what we called it?"

This was too direct a question to have been rhetorical, so Jen was on the spot. "Was that the thing you called Respect 2?"

"Not Respect 2," Matt replied. "Respect-Squared. The 2 was a superscript. But that didn't work either. And did we stop *there?*"

"Um, no?" Jen said, stalling for time. "Of course not?"

"You're right!" Matt replied. His excitement at the memory

was showing through. "Instead of spelling it R-e-s-p-e-c-t-[2] we started spelling it R-e-z-p-e-c-t-[2] – with a z instead of an s – so that it would seem more hip to the kids."

"Down," Jen said.

"What do you mean 'down'?" Matt asked.

"Kids don't say that things are 'hip' anymore," she explained. "When they want to say what you would say if you wanted to say 'hip,' they say 'down,' as in 'I'm down with that.'"

"Why would they say 'down'?" Matt asked.

"I don't know. They just do."

"If it's something that's hip, wouldn't it make more sense for them to say 'I'm "up" with that'?"

Jen's exasperation had gotten dangerously close to the breaking point. "Up, down, in, out…it doesn't matter! What matters is that the scores are still low!"

Nineteen years of marriage had taught Matt a few things, too, so he remained silent for a few seconds to allow the tension to abate.

Jen broke the silence. "So, mister fancy-pants management consultant, what should we do next?" Her now-playful facial expression took the edge off the question.

Matt played along by affecting an exaggerated version of his best consultant-to-client tone: "Here's what we're going to do, Ms. Wilson. First, we're going to remember that when things don't turn out as we'd like them to, it's not because of the people. It's because of the processes used by the people. Then we're going to identify those familial processes that are causing the low scores with the so-called soft stuff, apply best-practice improvement techniques to those processes, all the while tracking the key metrics we've identified so that we can make mid-course corrections as needed."

Jen knew that there was no turning back once Matt had built up this sort of head of steam. So she decided on the indirect approach.

"Okay, fine," she began. "But make me a promise."

"What's that?" Matt asked.

"No blind taste tests?"

"Fair enough," Matt replied. "No blind taste tests. And I think you meant double-blind."

"Whatever," Jen said. "And no offsites at the Holiday Inn?"

"Absolutely," Matt said. "We'll use our living room for any onsite offsites we might need."

It was all Jen could do to squelch another *Good-Lord-Matty-no!* reaction. She opted instead for getting one final concession.

"And no bucket brigades in the kitchen?"

"You got it!" Matt enthused.

"Okay," Jen said, screwing up as much fake enthusiasm as she could before adding, "Sounds like a plan."

"Sounds like a plan that's F-U-N!" Matt enthused again.

Jen gave a puzzled frown.

"Your store's slogan." Matt explained. "*Where F-U-N is Right There in Our Name.*"

Jen forced a laugh of recognition, adding, "You must be referring to my store's 'catchy' slogan."

Now it was Matt's turn to laugh a contented laugh. He was confident that the results of next year's F-MOS would be cause for a big celebration. Jen gave a patient smile borne of nineteen years of happily married life as she decided not to admit to Matt that her confidence level was considerably lower.

Ultimately, It Has to Do with Butterfly-ness

S O WE NOW KNOW that Matt Wilson is not only a high-powered, high-priced management consultant but that he's also a knucklehead.

After all, who among us would be so clueless as to do things like running an annual F-MOS? Or conducting a value-added flow analysis of the dish-clearing and dishwasher-loading process in order to cut cycle times by 30 percent? Or booking a meeting room at a Holiday Inn in order to hold a Family Quality/Six-Sigma Day? Or using their kids and their kids' friends as guinea pigs in a double-blind taste test to prove that Coke and Diet Coke taste different?*

Obviously, those are cartoonish examples. But here's the thing. I've seen smart, well-intentioned business people do things that are the logical equivalents of the approaches employed by Matt Wilson.

At this point you might be thinking: *The people who report to me are not my children! My colleagues at work are not my family!* And I couldn't agree more. But that's not the parallel I'm attempting to draw here. The relevant parallel lies in assuming that an approach that has worked for us in the past under one set of circumstance will

---

* Full disclosure: I actually did do this one, except for the part about it being double-blind. That would have been going too far.

Picture A   Picture B

necessarily work for us when facing a profoundly different set of circumstances.

Which brings us to Engagement and the rest of the Intangibles. As you will read several times over the next 126 pages, the first step in gaining a better "grip" on the Intangibles is to recognize – even embrace – the fact that the Intangibles are ... intangible.

As an intellectual proposition, this is easy enough to accept. It's also easy to accept that the Intangibles are important and that our ability to attend to them effectively affects business results.

As a visceral proposition, though, many (most?) of us have an innate discomfort in dealing with such matters. But we know that we have to *Do something!* vis-à-vis the Intangibles, and our strong bias is toward doing the sorts of things that have worked for us in the past.

In the great majority of cases, this is a perfectly rational approach. Unfortunately, though, the Intangibles exist on another plane, one that is not *ir*-rational but that is *extra*-rational – *other than* rational. And that extra-rational plane is different – profoundly different – from the rational plane. As a matter of fact, it's orthogonal to it, which means that if you're operating on the rational plane, those Intangibles won't be visible to you. They won't even cast a shadow.

To help get this discussion down out of the clouds, let me pose a question:

What is in *Picture A* above? (Hint: It's not a trick question.)

Answer: A butterfly.

Another question: What is in *Picture B* above?

Same answer, right? A butterfly. But while *butterfly* is correct in both cases, the two pictures represent dramatically different things.

The first one shows a butterfly that has been netted, euthanized,* pressed, pinned, matted, and framed. It provides very useful information about the butterfly: its length, width, color, signature wing patterns, and so on – its tangible aspects. So is it a fair representation of a butterfly? Yes.

But while the second picture isn't as clear about length/width-type attributes, it does a much better job of capturing what, for lack of a better term, might be called the creature's "butterfly-ness." The second picture captures the butterfly's "gossamer essence," if you will, an Intangible.

Another question: Which of the two representations of a butterfly is more useful in practice?

The answer? It depends. If you're a lepidopterist, you'd probably get more useful information from the netted/euthanized/pressed/pinned/matted/framed picture. If you're a poet, the butterfly alighted on a flower in a meadow would likely provide more inspiration as you ply your trade.

Yet another question: As a business person, which sorts of things are you more comfortable dealing with?

a) Things such as length, width, color, signature wing patterns;

b) Or things such as butterfly-ness and gossamer essence.

I've been posing this question in presentations and classes and seminars for years, and there haven't been a lot of people who have chosen answer b.[†]

The fact of the matter is that neither of the pictures is a butterfly. What they are, instead, are representations of a butterfly. Analogs to a butterfly. Artifacts of a butterfly. Proxies for a butterfly.

A similar logic applies to the Intangibles. The instant we think about, talk about, or write about them, we are no longer truly dealing

---

* Picture a bottle of chloroform and a *very* small handkerchief.
† And I have my doubts about the truthfulness of those who did.

with the Intangibles themselves. We are only dealing with representations/analogs/artifacts/proxies. The words we use are the nets and the chloroform and the pins and the mattes and the frames. There is inevitable loss similar to what we might think of in our tangible/mechanical world as friction loss, or the attenuation of a signal over time and space, or the loss of resolution between an original image and a photocopy.

That's the nature of Intangibleness; there will always be such loss. With that constraint in mind, let's now imagine a Spectrum of Intangibility, with the two representations of a butterfly anchoring either end (halfway in between might be a live butterfly in a laboratory setting):

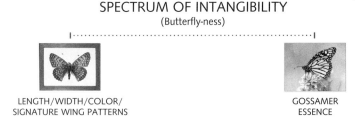

SPECTRUM OF INTANGIBILITY
(Butterfly-ness)

LENGTH/WIDTH/COLOR/
SIGNATURE WING PATTERNS

GOSSAMER
ESSENCE

Now let's consider three final questions:

1. Since words are the raw material we must use when attempting to deal with the Intangibles, and since there is always some loss of fidelity or resolution accompanying the use of those words, doesn't it stand to reason that we should strive to gain and preserve clarity and insight as to the meaning of the words we are using?

2. Since the words we use will determine just where on the Spectrum of Intangibility we're operating, doesn't it stand to reason that we should take great care in choosing those words, as well as the tone and context in which we use them?

3. Since many (most?) of us are far more comfortable operating on the tangible plane, doesn't it stand to reason that we have a bias pushing us toward the left-hand side of the spectrum? And that we should make a conscious and explicit effort to

exert a countervailing force to push things appropriately rightward?

Those are the questions we'll be examining in the pages that follow. And we'll use the Wilsons' story to see what can happen when those questions aren't even considered, much less answered.

CHAPTER 2

The Wilsons Tackle Engagement

It was Saturday morning, and the Wilson kids were off doing the kinds of things that high-achieving kids do on weekends.

Jess was at the dance studio for five separate rehearsal sessions: jazz, lyrical, hip-hop, tap, and her solo performance. (Jess was the only one in her dance troupe to be so honored.) This time of year, Skipper's Saturdays were devoted to bowling practice.

It was another set of parents' turn to do the driving (Skipper only had a learner's permit), so as soon as the kids had left the house, Matt began transferring a cache of high-powered-management-consulting items from the back of his SUV to the kitchen: tripod, flip chart, markers, as well as his all-time favorites – packages of sticky notes and colored dots.

He had asked Jen to gather up the F-MOS files and research reports from his office and spread them out on the kitchen table. Pointing to what Matt had dragged in from the garage, Jen asked, "Do we really need all of that stuff?"

"Tools of the trade, my dear," Matt replied. "Tools of the trade."

Those aren't the only tools in the kitchen right now, Jen thought. But what she said was, "Matt, I'm not your client, I'm your wife. And besides which," she gestured to the table, "haven't we got everything we need right here?"

Although this was a disappointing development (Matt did love his sticky notes and colored dots), he remembered a bit of the advice he had so often given to clients – "You've got to pick your battles." – and decided not to press the issue.

Another thing that Matt's consulting experience had taught him was that clients could often be anxious in the early stages of an intervention, so it was good practice to try to lessen the tension a bit by starting such sessions with a joke. "So," he began, "the Jesster is the only one with a solo in this year's recital. I guess that makes it a *solo* solo!" It was not the first time that he had used this line with Jen; he felt it was a sure-fire part of his repertoire.

Jen felt differently. "I hate it when you call her 'Jesster.'"

"But what else would I call her when I'm making a jest?" Matt beamed while making a set of shoulder-high quotation fingers.

"Yeah, right," said Jen, turning her attention back to the materials on the table.

Matt was undaunted. "Okay!" he said, clapping his hands, then rubbing them briskly together in eager anticipation. "Let's review the bidding from last night!"

Jen found this level of manic glee more than a little tough to take at such an early hour, but she bit her tongue.

"Right," she began. "We discussed this year's F-MOS results and the fact that we're still coming up short on the Intangibles."

"Exactly!" enthused Matt.

Jen's teeth applied just the slightest bit of additional pressure to her tongue as she continued. "We reviewed some of the steps we had taken in the past to get things to go more in the direction we want them to go."

"Move the needle," said Matt.

"What needle?" asked Jen.

"Ah!" Matt said. "I'm sorry. *Move the needle* is the term that big corporations use when they talk about getting different results. I shouldn't use that kind of jargon with you."

Jen didn't like being patronized. "Yeah, fine. Move the needle. Find the needle in a haystack. Get a tractor to pull the needle out of your..." She caught herself and bit down just a bit harder. After using a napkin to check to see if she had drawn blood, she continued. "Anyway," she began, with just the slightest exasperated emphasis on the first syllable, "we decided that the first Intangible we should work on is Engagement."

"Excellent summary!" said Matt. "Let's begin brainstorming some ideas for how to increase the level of Engagement around here! I'll capture them on the flip chart!"

Jen was not pleased. "I thought we decided not to use that thing? It's taking up half the room! Can't we just sit at the table and talk, and then write things down on this?" She held up a pad of lined notebook paper.

"Now, Jen," Matt began, in what he thought was a soothing, but was actually an even more patronizing, tone (Jen checked again; still no blood), "I don't tell you what the pH level ought to be when you're transplanting an arrangement of hydrangeas accented with fleurs-de-lis, do I?"

"Fine," Jen replied, unable to suppress a sigh. "Use the flip chart."

"Great!" Matt said, removing the cap from a black, flip-chart marker. "Let's brainstorm away!"

Jen quasi-enthusiastically dove in. "To move the needle on Engagement, we need to increase the opportunities for interaction with the kids. We need to find more and better ways to connect with them and make sure they feel more a part of things around here."

"I couldn't agree more," Matt said.

Jen looked as though she were about to say something, then gave an almost imperceptible shake of the head.

But "almost imperceptible" isn't good enough when there's a

high-powered management consultant in the room.

"You've got an idea," Matt encouraged. "Say it."

Jen began, tentatively, "Family meetings?"

Matt leaned in just as he had been taught in facilitation-skills training lo those many years ago. "Say more."

"Well, since Engagement means more interaction, I was just thinking that a family meeting would be a good way to go."

They were still in the brainstorming stage, so Matt didn't want to sound critical. "That's a great idea," he carefully began. "Do you mean a new family meeting in addition to the family meeting we have every night?"

"We do?" asked Jen, puzzled.

"Sure," he replied. "Our family dinners! That's why I always Skype in when I'm on the road with clients!"

"Oh, right," Jen said. "Dinner Skyping. The kids are big fans of Dinner Skyping. And do you want to know the kids' absolute favorite part of Dinner Skyping?"

"Absolutely!"

"They especially like the way you have us set up Skipper's iPad in front of your place at the table so that we have to scrunch in at the other end to make sure we're all in the shot."

Matt beamed. "And you were skeptical when I suggested it!"

Jen thought: *For such a hot-shot management consultant, you're not very good at picking up on sarcasm.* But she didn't say it. Instead she said, "I'm talking about *family!* You know, aunts, uncles, grandparents?"

Matt liked the idea. "Cousins, too?"

"Sure, why not." Jen replied.

"Just first cousins?" Matt asked.

"First cousins, second cousins. We can invite friends of the half-brother's nitwit third cousin's cable guy as far as I'm concerned."

Matt could be oblivious when it came to picking up on exasperation, too.

"Well," he said, "there are practicalities to consider. We have

to draw the line somewhere. And why do you keep dabbing at your mouth with that napkin?"

Caught in the act, Jen replied, "Uh, just a couple of toast crumbs, that's all."

Satisfied, Matt continued. "Another practical consideration is the size of the geographic area we want to cover. We don't want people to have to fly in for the family meeting." He picked up the F-MOS three-ring binder. Finding the section marked *Cross Tabs*, he read for a moment before saying, "We don't seem to get a lot of F-MOS responses from people beyond a fifty-mile radius anyway."

"We don't seem to get a lot of F-MOS responses from beyond the walls of this house," replied Jen. "What we're talking about here is the Engagement level of our kids, not your half-brother's step-uncle's godchild from Altoona."

Matt was puzzled. "Are you saying that it should just be the four of us? Don't our dinner meetings cover that? Especially

21

when they're augmented by our best-in-class Dinner Skyping program that the kids like so much?"

"No," Jen replied, not bothering to ask what on God's green earth Matt had meant by best-in-class. "I'm saying that even if we're only talking about our kids' level of Engagement, by bringing everyone together – from within, say, a fifty-mile radius – for a family meeting, that will engage our kids more fully."

"Okay," said Matt. "But if we're going to do this, we've got a lot of work to do. Agenda. Communications plan. Rent a space. Catering. Can you provide the centerpieces?"

Centerpieces?!?! was Jen's thought before she said, "I s'pose so."

"At cost?"

"Sure," said Jen. "Why the hell not."

"Nice!" Matt replied. His mind was racing as he energetically wrote on the flip chart. As the sheets filled up, he tore them off and stuck them to the front of the kitchen cabinets. "One thing the meeting has to have is breakout sessions. There's no better way to engage people than to have breakouts!"

"What will the breakouts be about?" Jen asked.

"We'll figure that out later," Matt replied. "We just need to make sure we have them."

"What else can we do other than family meetings?"

Matt had an aha moment. "Aha!" he said. "Skip levels!"

"What do we want Skip to level?" Jen asked.

"No, no," Matt explained. "Not Skipper levels. Skip levels! A series of meetings in which people normally two levels apart in the organizational hierarchy interact directly. Since the grandparents are going to be here for the family meeting, we should leverage that to make sure the kids have some time with them without us – skip levels!"

"Believe it or not, that's actually not a bad idea," Jen said. One could have been excused for detecting a drop or two of sarcasm. Unsurprisingly, Matt had not.

Matt added *Skip Levels* to the brainstorming chart. "What else?" he asked.

"Well," Jen said, "if Engagement is about interaction and connection, another way we can draw the kids in is by sharing with them the results of our businesses."

"Excellent idea!" Matt enthused. "After all, they've got skin in the game!"

This time Jen was more horrified than skeptical. "They've got what!?"

Even Matt picked up on this. "Calm down," he soothed. "That's just another big business expression. It means they've got a stake in things – that it's the money provided by our businesses that pays for the dance lessons and the bowling games and the what-not."

"Don't forget the iPad for Dinner Skyping," Jen said, switching from horror back to sarcasm.

"Exactly," Matt replied, oblivious as ever. "So once a quarter we should bring the kids in for a briefing on our quarterly results. Lots of charts and graphs and spreadsheets."

Once again, Jen was reluctantly impressed. "Wouldn't it reinforce Engagement levels if we also posted a few key business metrics on a daily basis? So that they would have a sense of how things were going in close-to-real-time?"

The flip-chart paper on the kitchen cabinets gave Matt an idea. "We could hang whiteboards showing the trend of each of those metrics on the front of all of the cabinets!"

Jen was surprised to find herself really getting into things. "We have to call a meeting with the kids to tell them about *this* meeting so that we can tell them about the family meeting and the skip levels and all of the other things coming down the pike to ensure that they'll be more fully engaged!"

Putting down the marker, Matt sat down at the table and took Jen's hands in his.

"If we do all of those things, there's no way they can think that they haven't been included…that they aren't involved… that there hasn't been a lot of connection and interaction!"

Jen was with him all the way now as she added, "When

they fill out next year's F-MOS, they *can't* say that we haven't engaged them!"

As she said this, Jen stood up. Matt quickly followed her lead and extended his right arm for the high five he assumed was forthcoming. But Jen's abrupt standing was less a burst of enthusiasm than it was the effect of three cups of coffee.

She made a beeline for the bathroom, leaving Matt with his arm frozen in the air, like a baseball pitcher at the point of release. Realizing what had happened, he awkwardly lowered his arm slot and patted down a non-existent cowlick.

"Good work!" he called to Jen.

"You, too!" said Jen, closing the bathroom door behind her.

CHAPTER 2a

Maybe We Need a New Word for Engagement

EMPLOYEE ENGAGEMENT is an undeniably good thing. The research demonstrating the business benefits to be realized by achieving a higher degree of Engagement is solid and compelling. Increases in profitability, productivity, growth, and employee retention rates are all very good things themselves and are all closely correlated with increased levels of Engagement.

There's a trap lurking out there, though, and it can prevent organizations from realizing those benefits. To help you avoid this trap, let me describe an experience I once had while working with a client. She was a corporate vice president who was preparing for an offsite meeting for the top 150 leaders in her company, and she had asked me to look over a copy of the draft agenda and provide some feedback.

The agenda items were pretty standard and straightforward: the just-closed quarter's business results, projections for the remainder of the fiscal year, updates on some key improvement projects, results of the latest employee opinion survey. Those sorts of things.

"At first glance," I said to her, "these certainly seem like sensible enough things to be covering in a meeting like this." But then I pointed to some words that she had penciled in. "I notice that you've added

Room A   Room B

Small-Group Breakouts here in the 2:00–3:00 time slot. What are people going to be doing during those breakouts?"

"We haven't decided yet," she replied.

Her answer caught me by surprise. "Then how do you know that breakouts are the best use of this hour?"

Now it was her turn to be surprised. "We always have a breakout module in these meetings. We have to get people *engaged.*" And when she said this, her tone suggested a sort of What-turnip-truck-did-this-guy-just-fall-off-of? bewilderment.[*]

In her mind, breakouts equaled Engagement. And while they might be a good vehicle for facilitating Engagement, they aren't, in and of themselves, Engagement.

To understand why that is, let's try a thought experiment. Imagine two adjacent rooms in a conference center with snapshots A and B above showing the activity in each room.

Question: In which room are the people more highly engaged?

Over the years, I've posed this question in scores of workshops and seminars to thousands of people, and the response is always immediate and virtually unanimous: Room A! Nobody has ever said Room B. Occasionally – *very* occasionally – I'll spot someone whose body language suggests uncertainty, and I'll draw out a third answer: Doesn't it depend?

---

[*] Yes, this was the inspiration for the Matt/Jen discussion on page 19.

Which, as it happens, is the correct answer. Why? Consider two scenarios based on what's going on in those two rooms.

Scenario 1

The people gathered around the flip chart in Room A are dealing with a topic that is not only of significant importance to the business but is also right in the mainstream of their day-to-day responsibilities. While they know that there is no guarantee that any of their recommendations emerging from this activity will be accepted, they also know that their recommendations will be taken seriously, that they will have been listened to.

At the same time, the people in Room B are being subjected to death by PowerPoint. The topic isn't particularly relevant to them, and a Google search on the speaker's name coupled with the words *Grand National Toastmasters Champion!* is unlikely to come up with any hits.

In this scenario, it's safe to assume that, yes, the people in Room A are indeed more engaged.

But now let's consider …

Scenario 2

The people in Room A all have the chance to speak their piece as the scribe diligently bullets their comments onto the flip chart. If it's a particularly high-powered breakout session, sticky notes and colored dots may even be involved. (Matt Wilson would approve.) But while all of this is going on, the thoughts running through people's heads are: *Didn't we just go through this exercise a couple of months ago?* And: *There's no way any of the higher-ups are going to pay attention to anything we come up with.* And: *This is just a waste of time and paper. I knew I should have clicked on DECLINE when I got the meeting invitation!*

Meanwhile, the speaker in Room B is covering a topic that may seem at first glance to be a familiar one, but he's doing so in new and thought-provoking ways. He's causing people to become actively aware of the assumptions they've been operating under when dealing with the topic, and he's challenging them to consider the validity of those assumptions. He also happens to be skillful enough to be able to hold the attention of a roomful of people seated auditorium-style on the kind of molded plastic chairs generally found in bus stations or at the DMV.

Who's more engaged in this case? Right. The folks in Room B.

The word *Engagement* is a common one, generally used to connote some form of interaction or connection. Recall the conversation between Jen and Matt on page 19:

> Jen quasi-enthusiastically dove in. "To move the needle on Engagement, we need to increase the opportunities for interaction with the kids. We need to find more and better ways to connect with them and make sure they feel more a part of things around here.

When two gears come together, they are said to engage. When a leader holds an offsite meeting with her team to kick off the new process improvement project, she puts a check mark in the Engagement column of her project plan.

And both of those are absolutely proper and sensible uses of the word. Here's the problem, though. The Engagement being talked about in those uses is very different from the Engagement referred to in the research showing the correlation with dramatically improved business results. *That* kind of Engagement can be defined thusly:

> *The extent to which a person invests incremental energy and effort in the task at hand*

It's not that the energy/effort definition is better than the interaction/connection definition, just that it's different.

At this point you might be thinking: *Okay. Fine. It's different. But aren't you just making a semantic point?* As a matter of fact, yes, I'm making a semantic point. But – *Warning: Second semantic point dead ahead!* – I don't think the word *just* applies here. As Mark Twain fa-

MAYBE WE NEED A NEW WORD FOR ENGAGEMENT

mously observed, "The difference between the almost right word and the right word is really a large matter – it's the difference between the lightning bug and the lightning."

Why is obsessing over definitions a really large matter when it comes to Engagement? Consider our leader who always included breakout sessions with offsite meetings. Before deciding to go this route, her thought process *might* have been this:

> *I want to achieve the kind of energy/effort Engagement that the research says will lead to better business results. One interaction/connection Engagement technique that can be effective in achieving such energy/effort Engagement is to bring everybody together for an offsite at the beginning of the project. Another interaction/connection Engagement technique is to include breakout sessions as part of that offsite. So that's what we'll do!*

And if that's what she was thinking, then we're good. But – let's be honest here – it's much more likely that her thought process went something like this:

> *This Engagement stuff is supposed to be important. We better have an offsite. And it's gotta include breakouts.*

Could this result in a higher level of energy/effort Engagement? Perhaps. But it could also lead to the kind of cynical reactions – *What a waste of time. I should have clicked on DECLINE!* – described in Room A, Scenario 2 above, where people are dutifully going through the motions while simultaneously rolling their eyes and sneaking looks at incoming texts and e-mails on their smartphones. Said another way, it could cause people to, energy/effort-wise, *dis*engage.*

The same argument can be made regarding the painfully boring Room B speaker in Scenario 1. In his mind, what he had to say was important, his logic was unassailable, and his PowerPoint slides represented a precise and comprehensive display of that unassailable logic.

---

* Recall Jen's sarcasm on p. 20: "The kids are *big* fans of Dinner Skyping."

CEB Corporate Leadership Council Model of Engagement

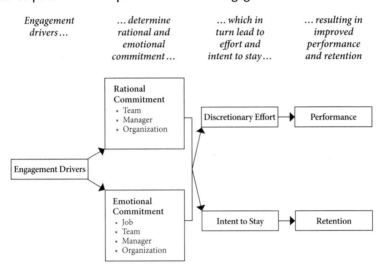

| Engagement drivers... | ...determine rational and emotional commitment... | ...which in turn lead to effort and intent to stay... | ...resulting in improved performance and retention |

Source: "Driving Performance and Retention Through Employee Engagement," CEB Corporate Leadership Council, Arlington, VA, 2004.

But he left his audience cold, because in preparing what he was going to say, he didn't give due consideration to how important and/or relevant it was to his audience – what *meaning* it might have for them.

There are various models used to illustrate Engagement. While the details of the models differ, they share a common characteristic – the need to account for both the rational and emotional dimensions of the human animal.

Pictured above is the model used by the CEB Corporate Leadership Council, one of the deepest repositories of insight about Employee Engagement around.

Note the essential role of rational commitment in the CEB model. It's there, in black-and-white. Without it, any effort to increase Engagement levels will fail.

That's why the impulse toward interaction/connection Engagement is a perfectly sensible one. With more opportunities for interaction and closer and more direct connection, information can be communicated more crisply and clearly. Questions can be answered more directly, and the ability to follow up – and read body language – can ensure that the question being answered is the one that is actually being asked. Cycle times can be reduced, since the pertinent facts that people need to do their jobs don't have to work their way through the normal and often byzantine communications channels. And the reduced level of friction loss resulting from this more direct connection will increase the likelihood that the information being received is closer to the information that was intended to be transmitted.

What it comes down to is this: The currency of rational commitment is *information*. So if the problem you face can be correctly stated as follows – we are not getting the right information to where it needs to be, when it needs to be there – then connect and interact away.

But what if that's not the problem? What if the question that people need answered is not What do I need to know? What if, instead, it's Why should I care? What does all of this mean to me?

What happens in such cases is the sort of thing that happened in Room A, Scenario 2. There was plenty of information flowing, facilitated by lots of interaction and connection. (Hell, there were even sticky notes and colored dots!)

But there was also a lot of eye-rolling and smartphone-checking and regret over not having clicked on DECLINE when the meeting invitation arrived.

Something essential was missing for the people in Room A, Scenario 2: meaning. Why is meaning so critical to engagement? Because the currency of emotional commitment is *meaning*. People want meaning from their work. They *crave* meaning. They *thirst* for it.

So the propelling question should not be: How can we ensure more interaction/connection? Rather, it should be: How can we ensure that we do the things necessary to bring meaning to the other person? Not to put too fine a point on things, but answering that question ain't easy. It certainly requires more thought and attention than simply penciling in the words *Small-Group Breakouts* on a meeting agenda.

31

Here's a (semantic) tip: When the words *engage* or *engaged* are used as transitive verbs – verbs that take an object – a red flag should go up for you.

You hear it all the time: "I've instructed Ellen to engage Greg so that she has the benefit of his insight and expertise." "Before moving on to phase 2 of the project, we fully engaged the leadership team."

But Engagement is not a series of activities in which people participate. It's a feeling-state in which people exist. There's a difference between what happens inside a room in a conference center and what happens inside the heads of the people inhabiting those rooms, and there's also a difference between mechanical, procedural inputs and the levels of energy and effort such inputs can generate. Those differences map precisely onto the differences between the two kinds of Engagement discussed above; that's why such usage should be a red flag for you.

Engagement is not a matter of leaders engaging employees. ⃰
It's about leaders creating the conditions necessary
for employees to be more fully engaged in their work.

Interaction/connection Engagement is important. In virtually all cases, the ability to achieve high levels of energy/effort Engagement will require the dutiful application of interaction/connection Engagement techniques. The trap lies in assuming that by achieving interaction/connection Engagement you have *therefore* achieved the kind of energy/effort engagement that will yield all of those wonderful business benefits. It's the "therefore-ness" that's the problem.

Were you able to keep straight all of the interaction/connection and energy/effort references in the last paragraph? Probably not, or at least not without a couple of re-readings.

Maybe what's needed is a different word to describe what this important but elusive topic is all about. After all, we don't want to be spending a lot of that precious effort and energy parsing the difference between interaction/connection and effort/energy.

⃰ *Engaging* is used as a transitive verb-form in that sentence. Did a red flag go up for you when read it?

What should that word be? We could finesse things by using phrases such as *Real Engagement* or *Engagement, Properly Understood*, but those are pretty clunky formulations. If there were only an *i* in *engagement* we could come up with a clever(?) rubric like: You can't spell *engagement* without m-e-a-n-i-n-g.

To be honest, I don't know what the word or phrase should be. What I do know, though, is that the act of searching for it can help instill a deeper, sounder understanding of what Employee Engagement – the kind of Engagement that all of those research results are referring to – actually is.

As Mark Twain might have put it, that would be a very large matter indeed.

CHAPTER 3

The Wilsons Tackle Empowerment

JEN RETURNED TO THE KITCHEN to find Matt immersed in the F-MOS report. He was frowning and slowly shaking his head.

"What's the matter?" she asked.

"I'm looking at the results about Empowerment," Matt replied. He shook his head a bit faster, more than a bit dismayed. "I…I…I guess I just have a hard time believing it."

"Hard time believing what?" Jen asked.

"A hard time believing that the kids don't know that they're empowered," Matt replied. "How can they not know that?"

Jen gave a sympathetic shrug.

"I mean, just last night," Matt said. "After dinner, we took the kids to The Eyes Creamery – and don't you just love their logo? The way the two eyes appear over the top of an ice cream cone? I'm not so sure I like the eye-*brows* being there, though. Depending on how the light hits them, sometimes it can look like two caterpillars crawling on top of a couple of chocolate chips, you know?"

"Focus, Matt, focus. Empowerment? The kids? Last night?"

"Oh, right. Anyway, we let them go to the window while we waited in the car. Wasn't that Empowerment?"

"And did we tell them what to order for themselves?" Jen said.

"We did not!" Matt added.

"No, we didn't," Jen continued. "I ordered the rum raisin. You had the butterscotch swirl."

"Delight."

"Excuse me?"

"You said that I had the Butterscotch Swirl. At The Eyes Creamery, it's called Butterscotch Delight."

"Swirl. Delight. That's not the point!"

"You're thinking of Sweet Treats. At Sweet Treats they call it Butterscotch Swirl. At The Eyes Creamery, it's Delight."

"Fine. I stand corrected. Now ..."

"Remember when they opened, and their sign had a typo so that it said 'Sweat Treats' instead of 'Sweet Treats'? Maybe they were going for something nouveau there, but Sweat Treats doesn't sound very appetizing, does it?"

"Focus!"

Matt caught himself again. "Right, sorry. Anyway, did we tell them that they had to order Rum Raisin or Butterscotch Swirl? No. Did we say that they could only order off of the left hand side of the menu? No. They have – what? Thirty-five, forty other flavors?"

"You're right," said Jen. "And they could have ordered any of them. Chocolate. Vanilla. Rocky Road. Tyson Knockout... although I think it's about time they removed that one from the menu. Black Raspberry. Cookies and Cream."

"'n," said Matt.

"'n?"

"It's Cookies 'n Cream not Cookies and Cream. Just like your store is Jonquils 'n Stuff."

Jen reached for a napkin and dabbed her mouth. "The point is that the kids were empowered last night, and they're empowered today." She pointed to the stairs leading up to the bedrooms. "Every morning, they pick out their school clothes from their own closets. Do we tell them what to wear?"

"Well," Matt began, a bit hesitantly, "sometimes we kinda do."

"When?"

"Remember that time about a month ago, when Jess came down the stairs looking a little, well...she looked kind of..."

"Slutty?" Jen's eyes blazed. "Is that the word you were searching for? *Slutty?!?*"

"I was going for something more like *age inappropriate*," Matt replied.

Jen was having none of that. "Do tell! At just what 'age' will it be 'appropriate' for your daughter to dress like a slut!?!"

"I'm just saying that you came down kind of hard on her," Matt said.

"You're damn right I did! And the next time she uses such poor judgment, the hammer's coming down again!"

"Do you think maybe that's the sort of thing that might make them forget that they're empowered?"

Jen was on a roll. "Empowerment is great. But if we go too far, we'll have anarchy around here!"

Matt was nonplussed. Stalling for time, he took a napkin out of the holder. "I think you've got another toast crumb right over here." He pointed to the corner of his mouth and reached across the table toward Jen's. "Let me get it for you."

She batted his arm aside. "And what about the other parents?"

Now Matt was completely bewildered. "The other parents?"

"They'll think *we've* abdicated *our* responsibility as parents!"

In his time as a high-powered management consultant, Matt had faced many situations like this. He knew that it was time to make a subtle adjustment to the trajectory of the discussion.

"Hey!" he suddenly declared. "How about those Sox? They won again last night! What's that...six in a row?"

Jen did not seem interested in a discussion of the American League East pennant race, but Matt forged ahead anyway.

"And how about that Pedroia? Isn't that little scamp something? Struttin' around out there like a little banty rooster!"

"I'm concerned about anarchy and abdication and you want to talk about the infield fly rule and barnyard animals?!?!?"

Thirty seconds of silence – a very long thirty seconds of silence – followed. As Jen's blood pressure began to come back down, she realized that she might have gone a bit too far. "Sorry," she said, then added, "I think I could use that napkin now."

It was still in Matt's hand. He began to reach across toward Jen's mouth.

"That's okay," she said, taking the napkin from him. "I can handle it."

Calm more or less restored, Matt spoke next. "I think we're in agreement that the kids are empowered, right?"

"Right," Jen said.

"Then the problem would seem to be," Matt continued, "that although the kids *are* empowered, they don't seem to *know* that they're empowered."

Jen could only nod, since the napkin was still in her mouth.

Matt pressed on. He had an idea to further lessen the tension. "What we have here," he said, "is a failure to communicate." And as he said this, he grinned and leaned forward in anticipation.

Now Jen was puzzled. "And you said that using that strange, nasal voice because ...?"

Matt leaned in even further. "Strother ...?"

Jen had no idea what he was talking about.

"Strother ...?"

Nothing from Jen.

One more try, one more lean. *"STROTHER ...???"*

Jen was more perplexed than ever. "Did we just start playing Password?"

"Strother Martin!" Matt finally explained.

"Okay. I give up," Jen replied. "Who's Strother Martin? Did the Sox just trade for him to back up your rooster buddy?"

"Strother Martin was the guy who played Captain in *Cool Hand Luke!* The guy who said, 'What we have here is a failure to communicate!'"

"Oh, now I get it," Jen said, reaching for another napkin. "Two things. One, please stop talking in that silly voice."

Although this bruised Matt's feelings, he quickly recovered when he heard what Jen said next.

"Two," she continued, "you're right. Or maybe it's Strother that's right. Either way, we *do* have a failure to communicate. We need to make sure that the kids understand that they *are* empowered."

Sensing that the momentum had shifted, Matt seized the moment. "So what are some of the things we can do to make sure that the kids understand that?"

"For one thing," Jen said, "we can make sure that we tell them more often that they're empowered."

"Good," Matt said, writing the idea on the flip chart. "What else?"

Jen was getting into things. "How about signs all around the house that say: 'YOU ARE EMPOWERED!'"

Matt built on Jen's idea. "We can make up stickers…"

Jen completed the thought: "…that they could put on their backpacks!"

"Yes, yes!" Now Matt was getting fired up. "Or we can use the old Uncle Sam poster…the one with him pointing!"

"And he can be saying: 'I want YOU…to be EMPOWERED!'"

"That's great!"

"Thank you!"

Matt jumped up, excitedly shaking his fists in front of his chest. "And we can glue letters to the top of their bathroom mirrors! Do you know what those letters would say?!?!"

"What would they say?!?!"

"They would say: 'I AM EMPOWERED!!'"

"Why would we want to tell the kids that you're empowered?"

"No, no," Matt explained. "It would be on the mirror! So when they're reading it, they'd be seeing themselves!"

"Brilliant!" Jen exclaimed. "It would be like the thought balloon coming out of their heads!"

"Exactly!"

Now it was Jen's turn to jump up, fists shaking. "How's this? We get some shirts made up...on the breast pocket it will say 'THE EMPOWERMENT COMPANY!'"

"I *love* it!"

"Thank you, but wait! I'm not done yet!" Jen said. "Right below the words, there would be cartoon figures of you and me and cartoon figures of Skipper and Jess and between us there would be a lightning bolt!"

"YES! A lightning bolt!"

Matt and Jen sat back down and beamed at each other. Matt thought to himself: *THIS is a High-Performing Team!*

"What about coffee mugs?" he asked.

"With the artwork from the shirts?" Jen asked.

"I've got something better!" Matt said, moving quickly toward a box that had been part of the car-trunk-to-kitchen cache. "Aha!" he exclaimed, as he pulled out a two-foot-long baton of rolled-up-paper.

He unrolled it to reveal an image reminiscent of the 1960s-vintage "Power to the People!" poster. But instead of saying "Power" it read "(Em)Power(Ment)." And instead of the iconic clenched fist, it showed four fists of varying sizes representing Matt and Jen and Jess and Skipper.

"I remember that!" said Jen. "It was from the Empowerment program we ran, what…three, maybe four years ago?"

Matt pointed to the one of the fists. "Remember how you can tell this is Skipper's?"

Jen shook her head no.

"See the ring finger?" Matt explained. "How it's all distorted just like Skipper's is from all that bowling? The way they really crank the ball now instead of rolling it like we did back in the day, when I captained the team…" As he said this, Matt had a far-off look in his eyes.

Jen leaned in for a closer look. "That's Skipper's finger all right. So you're saying this is what can go on the coffee mugs?"

"Exactly!" said Matt.

"Perfect!" said Jen. She paused, adding, "But the kids don't drink coffee, do they?"

"Why not? After all," said Matt, with a broadening smile. "They're fully empowered to do so!"

Jen stood up.

High-five time! thought Matt, as he started to stand.

But Jen brushed past him again, heading for the bathroom and calling over her shoulder, "Great work, honey!"

"You too, hon!" Matt replied, running his hand through his hair.

CHAPTER 3a

You Can't Bestow Empowerment

A S A LEADER, you know that you'll be able to accomplish far more through employees who are empowered than employees who habitually seek approval or permission before taking any action. But Empowerment can be an elusive concept in practice.

I once observed members of a senior leadership team as they listened intently as the vice president of human resources reported on the findings from a survey designed to measure Empowerment levels throughout the company.

The results were disappointing, and the team's concern was obvious. The business unit's president seemed most concerned of all. He was usually a stickler for staying on-agenda, but when the fifteen minutes that had been allotted for this discussion had come to an end, he said: "I know our time's up, but this is important. Let's keep at it."

Thirty minutes later, the president finally called time out. His reluctance was obvious when he said, "We've got to move on to other things." He turned to his vice president of quality: "It's clear that we've got some process problems that are causing people to think they're disempowered. Get your best Six Sigma people on it. Have them identify those process problems and pull together teams to fix them."

Then he turned his attention to his full team: "Let me be as clear as I can be. You are all empowered. I need you to go back to your people and make sure that they know that *they* are empowered, *too!*"

For just an instant, the vice president of marketing looked like he wanted to say something. Just as quickly, though, he decided not to. When the meeting adjourned, I managed to get a private moment with him: "You looked like you were about to speak up."

He nodded.

"What was it you wanted to say?"

"I wanted to say that we can tell our people they're empowered until we're blue in the face, but if people don't feel empowered, then they're not empowered."

"Why didn't you say it?"

He furrowed his brow and shook his head. "Nope," he said. "Too risky."

* * *

Empowerment isn't something that is generously handed down from the more rarefied levels of an organizational chart in a gesture of corporate noblesse oblige. Rather, it's a sense of assuredness that people at all levels of the organization have as they do their jobs. Here is a definition that captures that sense:

A feeling of safety while exercising judgment on the job

Let's parse things a bit more finely.

1. Empowerment is a *feeling* that the other person has, not an assertion made by the leader.

To tell people "You are empowered!" is a little like the old joke about the commanding officer telling the troops: "All liberty is cancelled until morale improves!"

The marketing VP's instincts told him that he should speak up. He didn't say anything because he thought it would be too risky; he

44

didn't feel safe enough to do so. In other words – and ironically – he didn't feel sufficiently empowered to question the boss's directive about Empowerment.

2. Empowerment is a feeling of *safety*.

One clue to just how empowered people feel is the kind of questions they're asking themselves when the time comes for them to take action.

They probably feel reasonably empowered if they're asking themselves questions like these:

+   Have I done my due diligence?

+   Is my decision consistent with our strategy?

+   Is it aligned with our business goals and our mission?

+   Is it up to the highest standards of responsible and ethical behavior? Does it accurately reflect our values?

+   When all is said and done, is this the best decision I can make for the business?

But here's a question suggesting a considerably lower degree of empowerment:

+   Will the boss rip my face off?*

Granted, that may sound a bit melodramatic, but I've heard those exact words used by people – *senior* people – who had been so beaten down by such treatment over the years that they felt like they had to look over their shoulder when choosing between Coke and Pepsi in the company cafeteria.

The "rip my face off" example may be extreme. The feeling behind it, though, is not uncommon at all.

---

* "And the next time she uses such poor judgment, the hammer's coming down again!" (Jen on p. 37)

3. Empowerment comes into play when there is *judgment* to be exercised.

Here's a concern about Empowerment that's felt, though not always voiced, by many leaders: "I'm afraid that what starts out as Empowerment will turn into anarchy."*

But Empowerment doesn't mean that anything goes. It has to do with exercising judgment on the job. And the most basic judgment to be made is knowing whether or not the situation at hand calls for judgment in the first place. You can't violate company policy and then explain your decision away by saying, "I felt empowered to do it."

In the course of a business day, people face a constellation of situations in which they may be called on to exercise judgment regarding what to do:

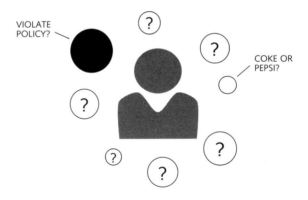

Empowerment is not a one-size-fits-all proposition. As a leader, you have to make judgments as to just where the boundaries of Empowerment are for each individual on your team. Let's say one of your team members has worked with you on many projects over the years, and you've always found her to be utterly credible and reli-

---

* See Jen's comment on page 37.

able. You feel safe in trusting her judgment in widely ranging circumstances. She gets a lot of white circles:

Another one of your team members, though, might not come up to such high standards.* He's a perfectly capable, perfectly competent employee. But there are certain circumstances in which you feel you need to keep a somewhat tighter grip on the reins.

You might want him to check in with you (gray circles) as he's moving through his decision-making process:

---

* Jess. "Age inappropriate" clothes. Enough said.

Or maybe checking-in isn't enough. You might want to approve the call (striped circle) before he makes it:

The key point here is that both team members can still feel fully empowered as long as two conditions are met.

First, they have to be clear as to where the boundaries are – what's black, what's white, what's gray, what's striped.

The second condition has to do with what happens when someone operates within those boundaries, but – as happens in the real world – things just don't turn out according to plan. (The white circle with the black X through it.)

Let's go back to the melodramatic extreme. If things don't turn out according to plan, and the leader rips the person's face off, well, let's just say that the selection panel for the Empowering Leader of the Year! award won't be dropping by for a site visit any time soon.

Here's a far more empowering reaction: "You did your due diligence and made a decision according to your best judgment. It didn't turn out the way we had hoped it would. It happens. Judgments aren't infallible. Let's find some time tomorrow to talk about whether or not there were any early warning signs we might have missed."

Of course, if things "not turning out according to plan" becomes a pattern . . .

. . . then the leader has a judgment to make. It may be time to rein things in a bit more.

But as long as there is clarity as to just where the boundaries are and reasonableness and professionalism when things don't go according to plan, a feeling of Empowerment can be preserved.

At this point, you may be asking yourself: Isn't this all just Leadership 101? And you'd be right. It is. The tricky part about Empowerment isn't that it requires mastering a new and complex set of principles. What's tricky is keeping clear in your mind the powerful connection between the diligent application of those Leadership 101 principles and the extent to which people feel truly empowered.

That picture comes sharply into focus much more quickly and easily when you're predisposed to take a step back and consider the world from the point of view of the other person. That will keep you from adopting an Empowerment strategy that consists of louder and more frequent assertions that "You *are* empowered!!"* In the process, you'll also find yourself spending less time trying to solve the mystery of just why people are so reluctant to forge ahead without feeling the need to ask permission.

Why? Because they feel sufficiently safe to do so.

---

* The "You Are Empowered!" stickers for the kids' bathroom mirror (p. 39) are based on something I saw first-hand in a Fortune 200 company's men's room. (Yes, they were in the ladies' rooms, too. I had a female colleague check.)

CHAPTER 4

The Wilsons Tackle
Trust & Respect

WHEN JEN RETURNED from the bathroom, Matt again had his head buried in the F-MOS report. But this time he didn't seem puzzled. He seemed upset.

"Matty," she began soothingly. "What's the matter?"

"I'll tell you what's the matter," Matt replied. "Trust & Respect is the matter."

Jen's eyes asked him to continue.

Matt was struggling. Despite his best efforts to keep his reply slow and measured, his emotions got the best of him. In fact, his eyes had teared up, so it was now his turn to reach for a napkin.

"I can accept the F-MOS scores being low when it comes to things like Engagement and Empowerment." He dabbed at his eyes. "But Trust & Respect? *Trust & Respect?!*" Another dab. "This cuts to the quick."

Matt reached for his wallet. He fumbled as he tried to pull out a stack of cards from the slot behind his driver's license. They were jammed in there pretty tightly, so he began to tug until the cards broke free and scattered across the kitchen table.

Sam's Club. Best Buy. A The 10th One's Free(ze) card from The Eyes Creamery. And the card he was looking for...

laminated, with a little notch at the top, and a headline, in gold type, reading: Wilson Family Values. Matt picked it up and held it up for Jen to see.

"They're right here on the WFV!" he said.

Jen nodded.

"Read them out loud," Matt instructed. "I want to make sure I'm not imagining things."

Jen held her hands out in front of her over the table, palms down, like a tennis line judge calling a ball in.

"Honey," she soothed, "I know you're upset, but..."

"Read 'em!" This time it was more a command than an instruction.

"Okay," Jen said, even more soothingly. She took the WFV card from Matt. "Where do you want me to start?"

"I want you to start with Trust and end with Respect," Matt said impatiently. He pointed to the card and added, "Right there. Right after 'Squeezing the toothpaste tube from the bottom' and right before 'No eye-rolling when Grampy Wilson comes to visit and insists on watching *Matlock*.'"

Jen nodded and read out loud: "Trust: Wilsons trust each other implicitly (except when age inappropriate outfits are involved)." She looked up at Matt and smiled. "Thanks for adding that."

"You're welcome," he replied. "I did take the liberty of doing some editing on your draft."

"And you were right to do so," said Jen. *"Slutty* would have been WFV-inappropriate."

Matt couldn't help but smile at this, so the tension in his voice was considerably lessened when he said, "Read the next one."

Jen looked at the card and continued. "Respect: Wilsons work hard to earn each other's respect every day."

Matt shrugged, eyebrows raised. "There they are. Right there on the WFV card. Trust & Respect."

"Yup. You're right," said Jen. "They're right there in black-and-white."

"Honeydew."

"Honeydew?"

"Honeydew," Matt explained. "Full-on white seemed too clichéd. I remember having a long discussion with the printer. We kicked around a few ideas. Honeydew. Ivory. Eggshell. Papaya Whip. I never knew there were so many shades of white, did you?"

Jen wanted to tell Matt to focus, but the digression was a small price to pay for the calming effect it seemed to be having. "Okay, honey," she said, ever soothingly. "They're right there in black-and-honeydew. Trust & Respect. Like you, I'm at a loss as to why the kids gave those such low scores on the F-MOS."

She paged through the F-MOS report and said, "I wonder if the survey is flawed."

Matt flinched at this, since he had designed the survey. "What do you mean?"

"Maybe the reason that the kids got the Trust & Respect questions wrong is that we were asking the wrong things," said Jen.

The pang Matt had felt at the criticism of his survey design skills was mitigated by the possibility of a way out of this dilemma. He found the Survey tab in his F-MOS binder and began to read aloud: "On a scale of 1–5, how would you rate the level of Trust in the WF? On a scale of 1–5, how would you rate the importance of Trust in the WF?" After then reading aloud the equivalent questions for Respect, he stopped and looked up: "What could be clearer than that?"

Jen shrugged a beats-me shrug. "I know, I know," she said. "But let's stay with the idea for a minute and consider the possibilities."

Matt went first. "Maybe they got the scale backwards and thought 1 meant good and 5 meant bad."

"I guess they could have," said Jen. "But wouldn't that mean that we did awful on the things like Selection of Cable Channels and Quality of Housing Facilities?"

"Hmm, you're right," said Matt. "Maybe instead of *ratings* they gave us their *rankings*. People get confused about that all the time."

Jen shook her head. "That would give us the same problem. It would mean that Cable and Housing and all the rest of the things we thought were good were all tied for fifth."

"Right again," Matt replied.

"What about this?" Jen said. "Maybe asking about importance skewed their responses. Maybe they think that we're great when it comes to Trust & Respect, but they don't think that those things are all that important."

"That's even worse!" Matt said. "That would mean that our kids think that Vehicular Options and Recreational Equipment are more important than Trust & Respect!"

"I'm afraid that this time you're right," Jen said. "Is it possible that they didn't understand what WF stands for?"

Matt seemed shocked at this. "What could WF possibly stand for other than Wilson Family?"

"I know, honey, I know," Jen replied. "But maybe we shouldn't take that for granted. I mean, we've been taking it for granted that our F-MOS scores would go up for Trust & Respect, haven't we?"

"White Flour," said Matt.

"White flour?"

"Maybe they thought *WF* stood for *White Flour.*"

Jen winced a doubtful wince: "On a scale of 1–5, how would you rate the importance of Trust in the White Flour?"

"It would be important to a baker."

"I suppose you're right."

"Or maybe it meant White *Flower,* not White *Flour!* Then it would be important to you when you're at your shop!"

Ignoring Matt's free associating, Jen had reached an important conclusion. "We need to rework the F-MOS survey before we run it again. Or at least we need to re-work the questions about Trust & Respect, since we're doing fine with the other stuff."

"Exactly!" said Matt.

Jen was pleased, not so much because of the decision they had come to, but because she seemed to have been able to talk her husband in off the ledge.

"Good job, honey!" As Jen said this, she stood up. Matt remained seated.

Jen was surprised. "Don't you want to high-five?"

"I thought you were going to the bathroom," Matt said, pushing back his chair and standing.

"No, silly," Jen said, holding up her right arm.

Confident that they had figured out why the Trust & Respect F-MOS scores had been so low, Matt and Jen Wilson high-fived. Exuberantly.

And this time there was no need for Matt to awkwardly run his fingers through his hair.

CHAPTER 4a

Toward More Practical Definitions for *Trust* and *Respect*

A s I wrote in Chapter 1a, the reason that this book has focused so much on words and shadings of definitions is that the words we use determine just where we're operating on the intangibility spectrum, and that in turn determines just how effective we can be in attending to whichever one of the Intangibles we happen to be dealing with at the moment.

SPECTRUM OF INTANGIBILITY
(Butterfly-ness)

LENGTH/WIDTH/COLOR/
SIGNATURE WING PATTERNS

GOSSAMER
ESSENCE

In Chapter 2a, I argued that Engagement tends to be equated with things such as wider and broader communication and increased opportunities for interaction. These are familiar notions right out of the canon of Good Leadership Stuff, things that we can point to and count and measure. So we're more comfortable when dealing with them, as a result of which we're more inclined to actually *do* them, placing us firmly on the left-hand side of the spectrum. But Engagement, properly understood, has to do with a feeling of investment in the task at hand. There's a fair amount of gossamer essence in that definition. So while all of that increased communication and interaction may help lead to higher levels of Engagement (note: that's *may*, not *will*), they're merely potential means to the end, not the end itself. It's only when we get out of our comfort zones by embracing the gossamer essence of Engagement that we can begin to move a few critical millimeters rightward on the intangibility spectrum.

The pattern is the same with Empowerment, as discussed in Chapter 3a. The going-in assumption tends to equate Empowerment with two things: (1) granting permission for people to exercise judgment on the job and (2) communicating to them that permission has in fact been granted. But it's only after embracing the more gossamer essence of Empowerment – a feeling of safety while exercising judgment on the job – that we again begin to move those few critical millimeters rightward.

This chapter is about Trust and Respect, which provides us with a different sort of challenge.

Let's be honest. There's a sense in which Engagement and Empowerment feel like contrivances. I think it's a pretty good guess that some of you reading these words can remember a time when Engagement and Empowerment hadn't yet made it into the leadership lexicon. So when those words began to pop up on our screens, they might not have been thought of as important new conceptual breakthroughs as much as they were seen as the latest "Next Big Thing" being foisted on us by Human Resources, which goes a long way toward explaining why moving them rightward along the intangibility spectrum involves such heavy lifting.

But we've heard about Trust and Respect all our lives. We've heard about them from our parents, our teachers, our clergy, and our mentors. We know in our heart of hearts that Trust and Respect are concepts that are big and deep, and that when we deal with them we're dealing with the *real stuff* vis-à-vis the Intangibles and not the latest contrivances cooked up by HR.*

So unlike with Engagement or Empowerment, we already *know* that Trust and Respect belongs over on the right-hand end of the intangibility spectrum. And it's precisely *because* we know that they're real, no-foolin' Intangibles that we're much more at a loss as to just what to do with or about them.

That's not a comfortable feeling. So we do some checking around to see how others might be handling things. Since it's not politically savvy to admit to such shortcomings, we keep this investigation pretty low key. As we gradually poke our heads out from our foxholes a bit further, it slowly dawns on us that no bullets are flying, since pretty much everybody else feels the same way.

This in turn leads to a kind of tacit collusion in fostering a shared belief that: "Hey, it's the soft stuff – the people stuff – that's the hard part. We're doing what we can but…" We may punctuate this by raising our eyebrows and turning our palms up in a "What are you gonna do?" shrug before reverting to where we're more comfortable – lengths and widths and colors and signature wing patterns.

In order to be able to check the Trust box on our Intangibles action plan, we might add a catch-the-blindfolded-colleague-as-he/she-falls-backward-off-of-a-step-ladder exercise to our next staff meeting. Or maybe employ a tell-us-all-something-you've-never-told-to-anyone-at-work-before! ice-breaker.

I once had a client who thought it would be a good idea to make eight-foot-high, three-dimensional letters – R-E-S-P-E-C-T – and have them line the drive leading to the company's main entrance. "People will see them every morning when they drive in!" he enthused. Since I knew him pretty well, I felt reasonably safe in offering this suggestion in reply: "Why don't you just hire Aretha Franklin and be done with it?" He got the point.

---

* See the distinction Matt made on p. 51 between "Engagement and Empowerment" and "Trust and Respect."

Here's another attempt that I witnessed first-hand. It was a large company that, like the Wilsons, had gotten disturbingly low scores on an employee survey when it came to Respect. So they launched a formal effort to boost those scores. (So far so good.) They even went so far as to create a video with substantial production values; as a large company they could afford the hefty price tag that comes with such a production. (We're still good.) The point the video was designed to drive home is that it's important to acknowledge the presence of others. (Still looking good.)

The video showed a typical conference room with seven or eight people seated at the table. The man at the head of the table – presumably the boss – began the proceedings by saying: "Before we get into our formal agenda, I'd like to acknowledge a new team member who has joined us. So-And-So has just transferred over to our team from the Thus-And-Such department. Let's make him feel welcome." At which point all the others either turned or reached across the table to So-And-So from Thus-And-Such, introducing themselves while offering a welcoming handshake.

This is not so good at all. Why not? Because while it's certainly a good thing to introduce oneself in such circumstances, doing so is just a matter of common courtesy. And therein lies the rub.

There's a principle from the legal world that I think applies here:

Expressio unius est exclusio alterius.[*]
(The expression of one thing is the exclusion of the other.)

A video saying that Respect is a matter of common courtesy is also implying that that's all there is to it. And we know in our heart of hearts that Respect is a bigger deal than that. "But," we tell ourselves, "corporate spent big bucks on the video, and I showed the video at my staff meeting, after which I used the talking points provided with the video to facilitate a discussion as instructed, so ..." It's at this point that we might wipe our hands in the universally understood gesture for: "That takes care of that! Done and done!"

---

[*] At last, those four years of high school Latin come in handy.

As a matter of fact, the company that used the video as part of their Respect initiative would agree that there was a lot more to it than that. But high-production-value video, plus talking points, plus instructions on how to use them in a staff meeting represent some rock-hard tangible stuff that has the effect of pushing us leftward on the spectrum. And like a kid on a swing, we're all too happy to accept that push.

Whereas with Engagement and Empowerment we don't really feel all that guilty about cheating over to the left side since we know those things are just contrivances cooked up by HR, we do feel at least a pang or two of guilt when the Intangible we're talking about is something as profound and important as Respect (or Trust).

Think back to our story about the Wilsons. They never really did confront the possibility that their Trust & Respect scores might have been low because Skipper and Jess didn't feel particularly trusted or respected. Instead, they began from the assumption that things were fine – "They're right here in the WFV!" – and then searched for explanations as to why the scores didn't come up to snuff:

> Maybe they got the scale backwards and thought one meant good and five meant bad.

> Maybe instead of *ratings* they gave us their *rankings*. People get confused about that all the time.

> Maybe they thought *WF* stood for *White Flour*.

Having persuaded themselves (read: rationalized) that the problem resided in the survey itself, they came to an important conclusion:

> We need to rework the F-MOS survey before we run it again.

… at which point they celebrated with an exuberant high five.

While the particulars of the Wilsons' behaviors might have been pretty far-fetched, the dynamic at work is, sad to say, all too common:

- ◆ Deep down, we know that things like Trust and Respect are important.

- ◆ But we feel discomfort at the prospect of having to actually deal with such soft stuff.

- ◆ We see a way out in the form of some perfectly reasonable, perfectly plausible action steps.

- ◆ We take those steps, updating our PowerPoint decks to reflect the progress(?) that we've made.

- ◆ Although we know, deep down, that we haven't really gotten to the heart of things, we take solace in the fact that nobody else seems to have done so either, because, after all, it's the soft stuff, and everybody knows that it's the soft stuff that's the hard part.

At this point you may be wondering why *Trust & Respect* were lumped together. After all, Engagement and Empowerment had their own chapters, didn't they?

That's a very fair question. As a matter of fact, it's a question I've asked myself every time (seven and counting) I've run across organizations that did precisely that: either talking about Trust & Respect as an inextricably connected pair – like Salt & Pepper or Gin & Tonic – or explicitly measuring Trust & Respect as a single entity on an employee survey.

But Trust and Respect are not only different from Engagement and Empowerment. They are also very different from each other. That ampersand is an important clue to the existence of an innate desire to not have to deal with such subject matter, to want to blend them all together into an indistinguishable whole, a.k.a., the soft stuff.

An inclination to lump them together is prima facie evidence of either sloppy thinking (a misdemeanor) or laziness (a felony). It's simply a respectable way of saying "And All That Soft Stuff," which we know, in our heart of hearts, can't be right.

Back to the Wilsons. While the F-MOS measured Trust & Respect as a single entity (bad), they did have them as separate items on the litany of Wilson Family Values (good). The problem lies in what was written on the WFV card. It was not only wrong, it was *exactly* wrong. Consider what they said:

- *Wilsons trust each other implicitly.*
- *Wilsons work to earn each other's respect every day.*

These words (minus *Wilsons*) are transcribed from actual company value statements that I've seen. While they appear to be unobjectionable, they are anything but.

A lot of things in life – especially in organizational life – come down to presumptions. Presumptions give us a jumping off point – a default position, if you will.

Do you *really* trust co-workers *presumptively*? I don't. If I find myself heading up a project team, and one of the members of that team – Person A – is someone whom I have never met much less collaborated with, am I going to "trust" that when Person A assures me that "I will do X by Y-date," that it's going to happen that way – especially if X is a mission-critical component of the project? No, I'm not. I'm going to build in an appropriate number of checkpoints with Person A along the way to Y-date to ensure that things are proceeding on course.

On the other hand, if Person B gives me the equivalent kind of assurance, and there is a long history of Person B having delivered on such assurances, then I may decide that I don't need as many checkpoints along the way. I will presume to have a higher degree of Trust with Person B than I will with Person A.

What I *will* give to Person A is my Respect, and I will give it regardless of what that person's pay grade is, what that person's background is, or what that person's demographic profile is. In other words, I will give it presumptively. I have a difficult time imagining anything less appropriate – and more damaging to the organization's soul – than treating people disrespectfully until such time as I have deemed them worthy of my Respect.

To get a better sense of these two Intangibles, let's remove the ampersand and take them one at a time.

* * *

Toward a More Practical Definition of *Trust*

Here's the definition of *Trust* that I recommend:

A feeling of confident expectation

Like Engagement and Empowerment, Trust is a feeling – something that cannot reside at the far left of our spectrum. But while we know that instinctively, we also know by now that if things get too far rightward, an equally strong instinct will snap us back over to the left. Fortunately, the other two key words in this definition – *expectation* and *confident* – provide a limit to how far rightward we need to move.

An expectation can be a very specific, knowable, pin-down-able thing. Think of the contract you signed when you took out a car loan. It was essentially a litany of what the parties entering into that contract could expect:

* That you would pay a certain number of dollars and cents each month

* What that certain number of dollars and cents would be

* The date on which you would pay that certain number of dollars and cents each month

* The address to which those dollars and cents would be sent

* The acceptable form of that payment: cash, personal check, bank check, electronic funds transfer

* What would happen if you were to fail to meet any of these stipulations

* What sort of indemnification you might have if the car were not to perform to acceptable standards

* A clear description of what those acceptable performance standards were

* Etc.

Of course, before you even got to the point of signing such a contract, the entity providing the funds for that loan – a bank, a credit union, the financing arm of the car's manufacturer – would have looked into your credit history. If it's good, you would receive the standard terms and conditions. If it's less good, you may have to pay a higher rate, if you get the loan at all.

Said another way, the financer would need an acceptable degree of confidence that you would live up to the expectations delineated in the contract. Confident expectations having been established, the financer would have a sufficient degree of Trust that the loan was a good one to write.

I once did some work for a company that did more than half of its business outside the United States. One of the fundamental questions that the company would always consider before entering into such an international contract was this: "Is there a legal system in place to which we can reasonably appeal if the terms of the contract are abrogated?" If so, the sales effort would proceed; the very existence of that functioning legal system would increase the degree of confidence in the contract, the set of mutually agreed-upon expectations. If not, then the contract, as the old saying goes, might not be worth the paper it was written on. While they might not walk away from the potential business opportunity, they might find other ways to ensure that they remain whole.

Think back to the simple example on page 63 where Person A assured me that "I will do X by Y-date." In the limit, I could have lawyered-up and developed a binding contract that included very specific criteria for what *do X* meant as well as a very precise definition for *by Y-date*: *by Friday, April 17, 2015, 5:00 P.M., Greenwich Mean Time.*

Of course, we don't do this in our day-to-day dealings with coworkers. It would be a terribly inefficient way to run a business. On the other hand, whether or not I accepted those "do X by Y-date" assurances depended on whether or not I was confident that Person A was up to the task, based on either my past experience or the recommendations of others who might vouch for Person A's reliability in such circumstances. And for this to work, I would have to Trust (i.e., have confidence in my expectation for) the judgment of that person who vouched for Person A. Not for nothing, but this sounds pretty similar to the kind of formal due diligence that the bank did before giving you the car loan.

So... how to create an environment of Trust? Three steps:

1. Adopt a more practical definition of Trust: *A feeling of confident expectation.*

2. Ensure clarity regarding expectations – that is, just what is meant by *do X* and *by Y date.* (NB: this is the responsibility of *all parties* entering into this implicit contract. Everyone benefits if all of the pin-down-able things have indeed been pinned down.)

3. Do your due diligence to ensure that you have an acceptable degree of confidence that your expectations will be met.

We enter into these kinds of implicit contracts all the time on the job. Trust – a feeling of confident expectation – is what's left over when the implicit contracting is done. Yes, it's an Intangible, which means that, much as we'd like to, we can never move things all the way over to the left on our spectrum. But while Trust itself is an Intangible, the three steps listed above are not. Follow them and you'll have a better handle on things related to Trust.

* * *

Toward a More Practical Definition of *Respect*

There's no getting around it. We know that Respect is a certified big deal. And like its first cousin, Trust, it's also a real, no foolin' item on the list of soft stuff. But we like dealing with things that are more rock-hard and tangible. We might even say that we find ourselves caught between a rock and a soft place.*

---

* Or you might even say this if you couldn't resist making a really lame joke.

Here's the dictionary definition of *Respect* that captures that big-deal-ness of our dilemma:

Esteem for, or a sense of, the worth or excellence of a person

Yep. That sounds about right. But it's also about as gossamer essence-y as it gets.

Let me offer a more practical definition of *Respect* that I think will help us resolve the dilemma:

Giving due consideration to the other

Let's slice things a little more finely:

- Definition of *the other:* Anybody who isn't you.

- The words *the other* sound a little odd, a little discordant, in this context, don't they? Wouldn't it be less awkward to say "Giving due consideration to others" or "to other people"? Yes it would, and that's the problem. Those phrasings conjure up images of groups of people. The image we need to conjure up is that of an individual person – the other.

- *Consideration* means just that. While you were saying or doing whatever it is that you said or did, did you stop to think about – did you consider – the effect it would have on the other? If so, great. If not, not so great. But the power of this definition is that it puts the measurement right where it belongs: in your head and in your heart and soul. You may be able to BS your boss, but it's difficult to BS yourself. (Some people do, however, manage to pull this off, which, although not particularly admirable, can be quite impressive to behold.)

- The word *due* is an important one. It's what keeps things from moving too far rightward on our spectrum. It recognizes the fact that we live in an imperfect world, one that calls for judgments and trade-offs. It also shifts the focus from concepts like *esteem* and *self-worth* to *effects on the business*.

An example. Suppose you received the following e-mail message from your boss:

"NOT what I was looking for!!!!"

That's it. No further explanation or context. Just those six words and four exclamation points, all bold-faced and italicized. What would you do in such a situation?

Well, if you had a really good working relationship with your boss, one that was informed by years of working together, you might have felt comfortable walking down to her office, standing in the doorway until you caught her eye, holding a copy of the e-mail at shoulder height by your thumb and forefinger and saying: "Having a bad day, are we?" At which point she might say, sheepishly, "Yeah. Sorry. I read your report right after returning from a pretty contentious meeting with *my* boss. You were the unlucky one who happened to be in the firing line at that moment."

You'd say okay, perhaps pointing out that the term *firing line* is never a welcome one when coming from one's boss. You and she would have a brief discussion to determine why what you had sent her had come up short. She would tell you that she had wanted you to include the latex sales to Vandelay Industries, at which point you would go back to your office and realize that all you now had to do was copy-paste part of a document that you had saved – it was in the Penske File – and that would be it. Crisis averted. Case closed.

(Quick aside: Things would only have unfolded this way if you had a feeling of confident expectation regarding your boss's reaction – that is, if you trusted your boss not to fly off the handle. While Trust and Respect are not the same thing, they are anything but unrelated.)

But now let's consider another scenario. You get the same e-mail, but the working relationship with your boss is less than hunky-dory. Under the circumstances, you conclude that this would not be the most propitious time at which to have an exploratory conversation with her.

So you decide to take another cut at things. It's probably going to take you the rest of the day to get this done. You check your calendar and see that your regular weekly staff meeting is scheduled from 1:00–4:00, so you send out a calendar revision to your staff, moving the meeting to the following afternoon. Your calendar now cleared, you dig in on the repair work for your boss.

You spend the afternoon on that repair work and send it off to your boss before leaving for home at the end of the day. Much as it pains you to have to do this, you keep your smartphone close at hand through the evening.

Sure enough, an e-mail from your boss arrives at 9:43 P.M. It begins as follows: "No!" Not a good sign, notwithstanding the fact that this time, at least, it was not in all caps, bold-faced, and italicized, and that there was just one exclamation point instead of four. Fortunately, there was more to the message: "I thought we said we were going to include the latex sales to Vandelay Industries?"

You stop and think – *Aha! Latex! Vandelay! The Penske File!* – then fire up your laptop, copy-paste the relevant section, and send it off to your boss. When you get up the next morning, you check your e-mail. Yup, there it is, in your in-box. You (anxiously) open it: "Thanks." Crisis resolved. Case closed.

Using our practical definition of Respect – *giving due consideration to the other* – who in this scenario was being disrespectful?

Your boss, of course. Had she taken a moment to think about how her original e-mail would be received, she might have included the bit about latex and Vandelay. By not doing so – that is, by not giving it due consideration – she chewed up your afternoon, thereby driving down your efficiency and productivity. Such are the business costs of such disrespectful behavior (not to mention an erosion of Trust).

Was anyone else being disrespectful? Well, if when you decided to move your staff meeting all you did was send out a calendar revision – no explanatory note – weren't you being disrespectful? Didn't this amount to doing the same thing to your people that your boss had done to you – summarily changing how they would be spending their afternoons both today and tomorrow? After all, they're responsible professionals, too. Presumably they had planned out productive uses for those times. And wouldn't this have caused a ripple effect for still other people with whom they had planned on meeting the next afternoon? Now think of the penalties in efficiency and productivity that can accrue to the business as this ripple expands. (And how people will file this experience away in their memories, to be consulted on some later date when determining the degree of confident expectation – a.k.a., Trust – they will have in future dealings.)

At this point you might be thinking: *In the real world, stuff happens. Things change. If someone is so rigid as to not be able to adapt to such changes, then maybe they've got some soul searching to do.*

And this is where the "due" comes in. Under the circumstances, you may not have had any choice but to spend the afternoon working on your boss's priority. But had you stopped to think about – to consider – the fact that your moving the meeting would be affecting "the other," you could easily enough have added a brief explanatory note to the meeting update: "Sorry for the last minute change, but I just got pulled onto an urgent project that will take up my afternoon. I've moved the staff meeting to tomorrow. Holler if this is a problem. Thanks for your understanding."

You can rationalize all you want to, but it doesn't absolve you from taking the time to give due consideration to the fact that what you do affects other people – individuals who have their own sets of issues and challenges and conflicting responsibilities to face while doing their jobs. At the very least, you as their leader can stop and take a beat if it will avoid making things even more challenging than they have to be.

I'll have much more to say about Respect in a later chapter. (Spoiler alert: It's sort of the key to all of this people stuff.) For now, let me offer a few closing thoughts:

- Had I pulled in to work one day and been met by a series of eight-foot-high-letters spelling out RESPECT as I proceeded to the parking lot, and then attended an 8:00 A.M. staff meeting that began with a video that seemed to reduce Respect to a matter of introducing myself to new colleagues in meetings like the one I was sitting in at that very moment, I *might* have thought: *Boy am I glad that I work for a company that is serious about Respect.*

But here's what I would be more likely to be thinking: *That video wasn't about being "respectful." It was about not being a very bad word that rhymes with brass pole. I'd rather they save the money spent on the video and the Stonehenge reproduction now lining the driveway and put it into a training program titled: "How to stop screwing up productivity by jerking around people's calendars."*

Here's a much shorter – and, considering the word that the Stonehenge reproduction spelled, far more ironic – way to say this: "I feel disrespected." And I bet I wouldn't have been the only one to feel that way. The urge to take action is a fine and necessary one. It's a place of business, not a faculty lounge. But our more practical definition of Respect – *giving due consideration to the other* – adds an essential step to the process. It forces us to ask: "How will what I am about to do impact other people?" The asking of the question, along with a good-faith effort at answering it, can save you from some serious missteps.

❖ Let's suppose that you were determined to make a video about the recent outbreak of failure-to-display-common-courtesy-by-introducing-oneself-to-new-team-member behavior you were experiencing. Wouldn't it have been more effective to show things from the point of view of the new person at the meeting? Show him sitting at the table, feeling the kind of awkwardness we all feel when we're the new kid on the block? Maybe get a close-up of him with a voice-over of the thoughts running through his head: "Should I introduce myself? Or would that disrupt the meeting?" Or: "I'd like to make a point here, but I feel kind of funny doing so." And so on.

By showing things from an observer's point of view, the focus – and the attendant lesson – was on the activity of introductions and handshakes. *Giving due consideration to the other* puts the focus where it belongs: not only on what we might do – or, as is the case here, what we might *not* do – but on its effect on the other.

Here's a short-hand way of maintaining an important distinction between Trust and Respect:

- Trust should not be given presumptively, but it can be earned.

- Respect should be given presumptively, but it can be lost.

Saying that Trust must be earned sounds more portentous than it actually is. When you get right down to it, it's merely another way of saying "past performance is the likeliest indicator of future performance."

To be sure, Respect can certainly be lost, and care should be taken – every day, as it happens – not to lose it. But everyone, regardless of rank or title or whatever other factor you might want to consider, is entitled – yes, *entitled* – to Respect (i.e., due consideration) as a basic condition of employment. To think otherwise is to invite the creation of the kind of Hobbesian environment – nasty and brutish – in which no business, much less its people, can survive for long.

CHAPTER 5

The Wilsons Tackle Values

Matt and Jen's excitement about having cracked the code when it came to Trust & Respect evaporated when they began to discuss the next disappointing F-MOS result.

Matt picked up the WFV card and began to study it. "I feel the same way about this as I did about Trust & Respect. How could the kids give us such a low rating on Values?" Then he added, hopefully, "Maybe it was a ranking."

"Focus, Matt," Jen said. She grabbed a napkin, then continued. "Just like we shouldn't take Trust & Respect for granted, we have to avoid doing the same thing with Values."

"Maybe I should have gone with the Papaya Whip."

Jen sighed and let this pass. "We should probably give the kids a choice between a clip and a lanyard during our daily Display-Your-Values! periods."

Matt was disappointed. "But lanyards are much cooler than clips!" he said.

"That might be so," Jen said, "but there's a practical reason for going with a clip."

"What's that?"

"When Jess wears a lanyard while she practices her dance

routines in the basement, she says that the card flops all around. Sometimes it even hits her in the eye."

"Oh," Matt replied. "Maybe we should get one with a clip for Jess."

"Good idea, hon," Jen said, patting his hand.

Matt stared at the WFV card. "Maybe we should look at rewording some of these items. You know. Like we need to work on the F-MOS survey questions?"

He placed the WFV card on the table so that they could both easily read it. "Let's take 'em one at a time," he said.

"Fine," Jen replied.

Matt read aloud: "'Value #1: Squeezing the toothpaste tube from the bottom.' Sounds good to me. What do you think?"

"Maybe it should say at instead of from," said Jen.

Matt said, "I agree," although to be honest, he wasn't really sure why. But he made a note of the change anyway.

"Value #2: Trust: Wilson's trust each other..."

"I don't want to talk about Trust anymore," Jen said, waving Matt off with her hands. "At least not today."

"Fine with me," Matt said.

"Or Respect!" Jen interrupted. "I don't want to talk about Respect anymore either."

"Okay," Matt said, making a note. "That takes care of numbers 2 and 3. Now on to Value #4: 'No eye-rolling when Grampy Wilson comes to visit and insists on watching *Matlock.*'"

Jen had a thought. "Maybe it should say 'No eye-rolling that Grampy Wilson *can see* when he comes to visit.'"

Matt nodded. "You're right. We don't want to be unfair to the kids."

"I mean, they *are* kids, and kids are going to roll their eyes," Jen said. "That's what kids *do!*"

"And the thing that matters is that Grampy Wilson not *see* it!"

"Exactly!"

Matt moved on to Wilson Family Value #5: "Love: And by

love we're not using a euphemism for trashy, smutty stuff, as in 'a *love* scene in a movie.' We mean, you know, the *real* kind of love."

"Maybe euphemism is too fancy a word," Jen said. "Maybe we should use something else."

"Like what?"

"I don't know. Like, maybe, *substitute?*"

"I like it. 'Value #6: No calling your sister "Isadora."'" Matt looked at Jen and said, "I gotta be honest. I've never really understood this one."

"Isadora *Duncan?*" Jen explained.

It still didn't register with Matt.

"She was a very famous *dancer?* And Jess loves to *dance??*"

A glimmer. "Wasn't she the one who was on *Jeopardy?*"

"Probably not, since she died like 100 years ago."

"No, no," said Matt, brightening. "She was part of the Final Jeopardy question. Or I guess I should say 'answer,' not 'question.' If my memory is right, there was something odd about the way she died."

"Yes, there was," Jen replied. "She always wore long, flowing scarves..."

"And her scarf got caught in the spokes of a car wheel!"

"Yes. That's right," Jen said, adding in a sing-song cadence, "Her scarf got caught in the spokes of a car wheel."

"And it broke her neck!" Matt said, triumphantly.

"You sound like you're happy that it happened?!"

"No, no," Matt recovered. "I just think that it's kind of cool... well, not 'cool' actually. But interesting. And ironic! You've gotta admit that it's ironic, don't you?"

There was a limit to Jen's patience, and it had been reached.

"And just how," she asked, "is that 'ironic'? Did Isadora Duncan design the open-spoked wheels that her scarf got caught in? And while she was working on the design, had she been repeatedly warned that people wearing long, flowing scarves might get them caught in the spokes, so that she might want to

think about a closed-wheel design instead? Because as far as I can tell, that's about the only way that *ironic* would apply here!!"

Since he was not quite sure what had just hit him, Matt decided to focus on the WFV card. Or at least that's what it looked like he was focusing on.

"Maybe it isn't such a good idea for Jess to be wearing a lanyard when she's rehearsing," he said. "You know, all those leaps and what-not. And the furnace has a fan to blow the hot air and all."

Jen decided it was time to move on to another, less depressing topic.

"Value #7?" she prompted.

"Yes, yes," Matt said, sneaking a dab at his eyes with a napkin as he tried to shake the image of a lanyard-garroted Jess. "Value #7: Honesty: And by *honesty* we don't mean when people say things like: 'And I'm being perfectly honest when I say this ...,' since that implies that the other things that they say might not *be* honest. We mean, well, you know…Honesty. *And we're being perfectly honest when we say this!* ☺"

"Should there really be a smiley face in the WFVs?"

"I dunno. I kind of like it," Matt replied. "Maybe it would be better if it read: 'And we Wilsons are being perfectly honest when we say this!'?"

"Yes!" Jen said. "That way it's more personal!"

"Done and done," Matt said. "Value #8: No calling your brother 'Junior.'"

"Yeah, that's a problem," Jen said.

"But he is a junior," Matt replied, plaintively. "I kind of like it. Makes me kind of proud. I wonder why he doesn't?"

"Do you really want to know?"

"Yes, I really want to know."

"He says," Jen explained, treading lightly, "that it infantilizes him."

"Skipper said 'infantilizes'?" Matt's disappointment had turned to pride.

"Yes, he did."

"Wow," said Matt, prouder still. "Then maybe it's okay to use *euphemism* in Value #5?"

"I think *substitute* will do just fine. Let's move on to number nine."

Matt read from the WFV card: "Value #9: Listening: And by *listening* we don't mean simply the vibration of the ear drum that sends a signal to the auditory nerve that then transmits that signal to the brain that in turn translates it into the phenomenon we call 'sound'…we mean, you know, actually *listening* to the other person."

"Isn't all of that talk about the ear and the brain a bit confusing?" Jen asked.

"Maybe we should add a diagram?" Matt suggested.

"Would there be room?"

"There would be if we doubled the size of the card and then folded it in half."

Jen liked it. "Perfect!" she said.

"Once again, done and done!" said Matt. "Time to move on to number ten."

Since this was the last Value on the WFV card, Matt used his best, most authoritative voice when he read it: "Value #10: No telling Nana Pepitone that her Cabbage and Penne Surprise isn't as delicious as it used to be."

This time it was Jen's turn to dab at her eyes with a napkin. "This one is important to me," she said, her voice breaking ever so slightly. "My mother has cooked Cabbage and Penne Surprise ever since I can remember. She's very, very proud of it."

Now it was Matt's turn to do the hand-patting. "As well she should be," he said.

"And I'm very grateful to you for editing what Skipper had submitted when we were developing these Value statements," said Jen, giving Matt a sincere, loving smile.

"Well," Matt said, "I just figured that 'isn't as delicious as it used to be' was better than 'sucks.' You know, kind of like the 'slutty' thing on the other one." Then he quickly added, "And it isn't just a wordsmithing change. Your mother's Cabbage and Penne Surprise doesn't suck at all!"

"Thanks, dear," Jen said, with an even more loving smile. "You're a real sweetie."

"You spelled that correctly in your head, didn't you? You did mean *sweetie* and not *sweatie?*"

It took an instant for Jen to get the joke. She laughed and said, "Yes…SWEE-tie!"

"Back to work," he said, quite pleased with himself about his little word-play. "Are there any changes we should make to this one?"

Jen said, "Should we change it from a negative to a positive? So instead of saying don't tell my mother that it's not as delicious, maybe we could say, 'Be sure to tell Nana Pepitone that her Cabbage and Penne Surprise is as delicious as ever.'?"

"I'm not so sure about that," Matt said, pointing to WFV #5: Honesty.

Jen nodded. "You're right. But this one means so much to me."

Now Matt nodded. "I know it does. I think the way it's worded now is just fine."

"Okay," Jen said, adding mischievously, "Sweaty!"

Matt played along. He held his arm up.

"I *don't* want to high five!" Jen said.

"Who's high-fiving?" Matt replied. "I'm just checking my underarms for stains!"

Jen laughed. Then she grabbed a fistful of napkins and offered them to Matt. "Here," she said, gesturing toward his left underarm. "You might need these."

They shared a laugh. A boisterous, loving laugh. A boisterous, loving, oblivious-as-ever laugh.

CHAPTER 5a

Company Values, Human Nature, and Gresham's Law

WE LEARNED A LOT about the WFV – Wilson Family Values – in the last section, didn't we? After all, it was all right there in black-and-honeydew:

1. Squeezing the toothpaste tube at the bottom.

2. Wilsons trust each other implicitly.

3. Wilsons work hard to earn respect every day.

4. No eye-rolling that Grampy Wilson can see when he comes to visit and insists on watching *Matlock*.

5. Love: And by *love* we're not using a euphemism for trashy, smutty stuff as in "a love scene from a movie." We mean, you know, the *real* kind of love.

6. No calling your sister "Isadora."

7. Honesty: And we Wilsons are being perfectly honest when we say this! ☺

8. No calling your brother "Junior."

9. Listening: And by *listening* we don't mean simply the vibration of the ear drum that sends a signal to the auditory nerve that

then transmits that signal to the brain that in turn translates it into the phenomenon we call "sound" … we mean, you know, actually *listening* to the other person.

10. No telling Nana Pepitone that her Cabbage and Penne Surprise isn't as delicious as it used to be.

The trouble is, what we learned about the Wilson's values didn't come from the WFV card as much as it came from Matt's and Jen's obviously heartfelt discussions about what was on the card, not to mention what we had learned about the Wilsons from previous chapters.

We know that Matt and Jen care deeply about each other and about their kids. See Matt's anguish about the low scores for Trust & Respect on page 51. ("I can accept the F-MOS scores being low when it comes to things like Engagement and Empowerment. But Trust & Respect? *Trust & Respect?* This cuts to the quick.") See Jen's gratitude at Matt's editorial judgment on page 79. ("Thanks, dear. You're a real sweetie.") See both of them trying to put themselves in Skipper's and Jess's shoes on page 74. (Matt nodded. "You're right. We don't want to be unfair to the kids." "I mean, they *are* kids …," Jen said.)

Granted, some of the items listed on the WFV cards are pretty silly, such as the one about how to squeeze the toothpaste tube, or Grandpa Wilson's wanting to watch *Matlock*, or Nana Pepitone's Cabbage and Penne Surprise. But even those are about being sensitive to how one family member's actions might affect the feelings of another.

And while the painfully detailed descriptions of what *love* and *listening* really mean are kind of tortured in WFV #5 and #9, they also bespeak a desire to underscore just how important those Values are in the Wilson family.

But the Wilsons are just four people, so it's fairly easy to get a sense of just what their Values are, even in the admittedly broad and cartoonish way their exploits have been described in these pages. We can read between the lines of the WFV card and draw these deeper inferences because we've seen Matt and Jen in action, and clichéd though it may sound, actions do indeed speak louder than words.

In real business life, however, things are considerably more complex. Those actions are occurring all over the organization, far beyond the visible horizons of any individual or small group. Consequently, the desire to promulgate a clear and shared sense of what those Values are is a perfectly rational and sensible one. Alas, there are pitfalls to be avoided when doing so.

Herewith, two assertions:

1. A company's Values are important.

2. Most people in leadership positions agree with assertion #1 and try to do their best to ensure that their behaviors are consistent with those Values.

If you disagree with #1, you're in the wrong book. If you disagree with #2, you're in the wrong job.

There are a number of definitions for Values out there, and they generally invoke words such as *moral compass*, *guiding principles*, *operating philosophies*, *foundation for decision making*, and *cultural DNA*.

All of these are good and sensible ways to describe Values. But let me suggest another definition:

What really matters around here

I like it because it's a little less lofty, a little more down-to-earth.

Regardless of the importance of Values or the definition that's used, there are ways that good-faith efforts to promulgate Values throughout an organization can be ineffectual – and maybe even do damage – and they're rooted in the following principle: "Bad money drives out good." That's the colloquial statement of Gresham's Law, which comes from the world of economics.

According to Gresham's Law, when the currency is inflated in Year X, the dollar you saved in Year X−1 loses value. As inflation continues in Year X+1, the value of your Year X−1 dollar drops even further. And on it goes, with more and relatively cheaper dollars chasing the same number of goods and services, the newer dollars crowding out the older ones, and the currency becoming further debased. Said another way, bad money has driven out good.

Think about the little exercise we've all done, where we say a common word over and over and over and over and over again. What happens after the tenth or twelfth time you say the word? Right. It begins to sound like nonsense. It loses its meaning. What do you suppose happens to the word *Values* when it begins to appear on too many walls, and on too many flat-screens, and in too many webcasts, and on too many meeting agendas? When too many invocations of *Values* are chasing the same number of ears and the same number of hearts and minds?

At what point do you get to "too many"? There's no hard and fast answer. The important thing is to recognize that such a point exists and to wrestle with the challenge of locating it. Merely doing that will help you avoid this pitfall. And, human nature being what it is, it will also differentiate you from most other companies.

* * *

Company Values *are* important. They should be invoked with care so as to preserve their no-foolin'-this-is-a-big-deal status. Here are two ways to promulgate your company Values:

1. Live each day making sure that you are guided by those Values, using them to help make tough decisions and break ties, setting an example with your Values-driven behavior, applying them as a screen when making new hires, and making sure that the people over whom you have influence are doing similar things in their spheres of influence.

2. Stick 'em on a poster.

Granted, option #2 is a bit of a caricature. And I'm not suggesting that you would be so tin-eared as to promote company Values by emblazoning them onto one-size-fits-all baseball caps, coffee mugs, or Frisbees. (Or at least I hope you're not. Rule of thumb: if the word *tchotchke* can be applied, don't do it.) What I *am* suggesting is that the temptation to just "stick 'em on a poster" would appear to be a powerful one, given how frequently it – or its equivalent – is employed as a Values-promulgation tactic in many organizations.

Suppose you were investing the time and effort necessary to treat your company's Values as something due the kind of care and respect that's embodied in option #1 above. But when you looked around, you saw that everyone else was just stickin' 'em on posters? What's more, that approach seemed to be perfectly fine. Nobody was being called to account for taking the lazy way out.

Human nature being what it is, wouldn't your next thought likely be: *Where's the phone number of that printer?*

When you think about it, Gresham's Law applies here, too. But instead of the currency being inflated by too many references to Values, this time the currency is being debased by what might be thought of as "counterfeit" activities: printing posters instead of manifesting behaviors.

* * *

There are two ways that our working definition of Values – *what really matters around here* – can be interpreted, and it depends on how the adverb *really* is employed.

In one interpretation, *really* is used as what linguists call an intensifier: "Yes, X matters. As a matter of fact, it *really* matters." In the other interpretation, *really* is used as a discriminator: "Sure we *say* that X matters. But now let me tell you what *really* matters around here."

See the difference? It's important because people are very good at sensing the existence of any gaps between purported Values and actual behaviors. And human nature being what it is, the louder we turn up the volume on the statements of those Values, the more rapidly their antennae will begin to twitch.

At this point you might be thinking: *Good. I welcome the challenge. I want people to hold me to those Values!* And that's an admirable position to take. But when people perceive a say-do gap, there are two ways they can go. They can think: *Hmmm. What George just said doesn't seem to be consistent with our Values. That's not like him. I need to talk to George to make sure that I'm not misunderstanding.* Or they can think: *What a hypocrite!*

Human nature being what it is, guess which option they're more likely to choose? Right. The bad interpretation (What a hypocrite!) will tend to drive out the more benign interpretation (That's not like George.). As people begin to compare notes – and they will – the cynicism will spread, and that can be fatal to organizational health. So soft-pedal the talking. Focus on the doing.

* * *

I once found myself listening to the following rant from someone who worked in a client's organization. He was not in a position of formal leadership, but he was a well-respected and influential individual contributor.

> All of this talk about Values is getting me more and more spun up. If our Values are as important as we say they are, then we ought to stop spending so much time and money talking about them and more time living them! And besides which, I don't give two s***s about "Company Values." The only relevance they have to me is so I can decide whether or not it's a place I want to work. I don't get my Values from my employer. I get them – I *got* them – from my parents, and my priests, and my mentors. My Values are deeply rooted in my heart and soul, not clipped to a lanyard that's hanging around my neck.

No, I don't think it's the intent of any reasonable leader to equate company Values with personal Values. (At least I hope it isn't.) But unless care and effort is expended on keeping that distinction clear, it can appear that the two are being conflated. Be explicit about the distinction between the company's Values and an individual's Values. Otherwise – and given human nature and Gresham's Law – the bad interpretation will drive out the good, people will assume the worst, their list of personal Values will always trump the company's Values, and that will lead to rants like the one above.

* * *

It was in the 1980s that businesses of all stripes began paying much closer attention to the Intangibles, in large part prompted by the 1982 publication of *In Search of Excellence*, the huge business best-seller authored by Tom Peters and Bob Waterman.

My employer at the time, a Boston-area electronics company, was no exception, having launched a major Shared Values initiative. Make no mistake, this initiative was anything but lip service. It was energetically led by Bill, the CEO, who, along with the full roster of company executives, devoted untold hours to identifying, defining, and wordsmithing those shared Values. Some of this work was done in closed sessions with just Bill and his leadership team. Some was done in focus groups that included representatives from throughout the company – all functions, all levels, all locations, all demographic slices. Some of it was Bill's own, internal musings.

It was clear to everyone in the company that the Shared Values initiative was being taken seriously. What was also clear to everyone, though, was that it was taking a long time – a very long time – to complete.

About six months into the effort, there happened to be a week-long meeting of all company marketing personnel. As was his wont, Bill opened the meeting with gracious welcoming remarks, and as had become his wont over the past six months, he used this platform to update everyone on where things stood vis-à-vis Shared Values.

One of the executives in attendance at this meeting was Brian, the vice president with P&L responsibility for the product line that was being counted on to pull the company out of a prolonged sales slump. Now, it was an open secret that Brian was under considerable pressure to accelerate the pace of development of his product line's new model and bring it to market. So when, at the end of Bill's Shared Values update, Brian raised his hand and said, "All of this planning and development are great, Bill, but when are you going to ship the damn thing?" there was a two-beat pause, followed by explosive laughter from all corners of the room. (Fortunately for Brian, one of the people laughing the hardest was Bill.)

Don't get me wrong. The fact that Bill and company were taking the company's Values so seriously is a seriously good thing. But the explosive laughter that followed Brian's irreverent question tells us that, at a gut level, people understood that there was something profoundly amiss with the approach being taken, that in the process of doing all of that tweaking and polishing and honing, some of the real value of the exercise was leeching out.* More than a little ironic, that.

The Wilsons fell into the same trap as Bill et al., focusing on doing some tweaking to the WFV and the F-MOS rather than taking a step back and a deep breath and realizing that Values aren't stipulated, they're lived. So unless you have the moral authority of Moses carrying down the tablets from Mt. Sinai, go easy on the *ex cathedra pronunciamentos* and WFV-card-like tactics. They're too far left on our intangibility spectrum. Because if there's one Intangible where utmost diligence is called for when it comes to maintaining its gossamer essence, it's Values.

* * *

Let's wrap this chapter up with three specific, prescriptive steps you can take to avoid the various pitfalls associated with company Values:

1. When it comes to the promulgation of company Values, give yourself a budget of precisely $0. Of course this is fanciful.

---

* The very fact that Brian could ask such a question and that the people in the room (including Bill – come to think of it, *especially Bill!*) could laugh so openly tells us more about the company's Values than anything that could be placed on whatever the early-'80s equivalent of a flat-screen might have been.

At some point you're likely to have to open up the check-book. But by starting from the assumption that you will have to invest some real sweat-equity in the effort, you'll be a lot less likely to take the lazy – and ultimately far more costly – way out.

2. Instead of you telling the people you lead what your orga-nization's operating Values are, ask them to tell you. This is difficult to do if you already have a Values promulgation pro-gram in place, since, human nature being what it is, people will be inclined to give you what they think you want to hear (i.e., what it says on the Values posters and flat-screens) rather than what they'd really like to say. It's here that our definition of Values that uses the adverb as a discriminator – *what* really *matters around here* – comes in handy. It may take some do-ing, but if you can persuade them that you really* want to hear their answer, it's well worth doing.

3. Make clear that the reason that you're talking about Values is not that you expect people to change their own set of Val-ues. Rather, it's so that they can do some self-calibration as to whether or not this is the place for them.

---

* *Really* is here being used as a combination of intensifier and discriminator.

CHAPTER 6

The Wilson Family Meeting
(Ten Days Later)

Jᴇss ᴀɴᴅ Sᴋɪᴘᴘᴇʀ would be home from school any minute now, so Matt and Jen took a step back to inspect their own handiwork one last time.

It was really quite remarkable. In the few short hours since the kids had left for school that morning, the Wilsons' warm, cozy living room had been transformed to exude the stainless-steel professionalism of a middle-of-the-road corporate conference center – just the effect Matt had been going for.

Stretched across the living room's entrance, just below the dentil molding, was a banner reading:

YOU CAN'T SPELL *INTANGIBLES* WITHOUT A-B-L-E!

In an especially nice touch, the Wilsons' four-fisted "(Em) Power(Ment) to the People!" illustration – Skipper's distorted ring finger and all – appeared in the banner's lower right hand corner.

Floral arrangements – "Courtesy of Jen's Jonquils 'n Stuff!" – stood sentry on each side of the entrance. Next to one arrangement was a new lanyard for Skipper. Next to the other was a clip for Jess.

Just inside, Matt had found a use for two of his high-powered management consulting tripods. One supported a foam-core-backed poster reading: "Next Year's F-MOS Will Be The F-MOS(T)!" The other displayed a blown-up version of the new WFVs.

Right alongside the WFV poster was a long table with an array of items evoking elements of the WVFs themselves:

+ A boxed set of *Matlock* DVDs.

+ A portrait of Jess in a dance outfit (lyrical) next to a photograph of Isadora Duncan, scarf flowing, the universal symbol for "DO NOT" (red circle bisected at a 45-degree angle by red slash) over Isadora's face.

+ A picture of Junior Samples with the same "DO NOT" symbol across *his* face. (This one was pretty cryptic, but Matt had really loved watching *Hee-Haw* when he was a kid.)

+ An EMPOWERMENT COMPANY shirt.

+ A coffee mug featuring the four-fisted (Em)Power(Ment) logo.

+ A sign reading: "RATINGS ≠ RANKINGS." (Jen had argued against this, but Matt had prevailed. He thought it would serve as a subtle reinforcement for when the kids filled out the next year's F-MOS survey. To serve as further reinforcement, a copy of this year's F-MOS report was directly under the sign, with "(T)" penciled in so that it now read "F-MOS(T).")

+ And in a final and inspired touch, there was also a generous portion of Nana Pepitone's Cabbage and Penne Surprise (Jen always kept some in the freezer)... with a place setting for one... Skipper's iPad set up next to it in Dinner Skyping position... and a picture of Matt displayed on the iPad's screen.

Matt and Jen heard the exhaling sigh of a school bus's air

92

brakes. *Jess and Skipper would be walking through the door in a matter of seconds!*

They rushed to take up their positions just inside the front door and could hear the kids' good-natured teasing getting louder and louder as Jess and Skipper made their way up the front walk.

The door opened. Matt and Jen didn't say a word. Instead, they made a broad *Go-on-in!* gesture toward the living-room-cum-conference-center to their left.

Jess and Skipper turned to their right and saw the banner and the floral arrangements and the rest of the displays that their mom and dad had – obviously lovingly – laid out. They smiled, then turned back to their mom and dad to give nods of approval. Then they held out their arms – Jess toward Matt and Skipper toward Jen – in the family's unmistakable signal that it was time for a group hug.

The four Wilsons gathered together in a tight bond (literally and figuratively). Matt and Jen stole a look at each other. The expressions on their faces could mean only one thing: We did it!

And they had. Even though it hadn't been for any of the F-MOS-inspired reasons that they thought they had.

CHAPTER 6a

It's Not About Action Steps

THIS WILL BE SHORT AND SWEET but not *too* sweet, since the last chapter ended with a scene so treacly that you probably should check with your doctor to make sure that you're not on the edge of hyperglycemic shock after reading it:

> The four Wilsons gathered together in a tight bond (literally and figuratively). Matt and Jen stole another look at each other. The expressions on their faces could mean only one thing: We did it!

But the cryptic concluding paragraph is intended to sour things up a bit:

> And they had. Even though it hadn't been for any of the F-MOS-inspired reasons that they thought they had.

What is the "it" that Matt and Jen "did"? The evidence at hand suggests that they had done no less than create a loving and closely-knit family.

Was it the Dinner Skyping and the WFV cards and the serving of Cabbage and Penne Surprise displayed in the living-room-cum-conference-center? Yes and no.

It wasn't those tangible actions themselves that did it. In fact, Skipper and Jess sensed that those actions were kind of silly, even goofy. (Adolescents are very good at sensing goofiness.) It's also why they had habitually given such low scores to the Intangibles on the annual F-MOS, since the F-MOS itself had been a cue to consider the Intangibles on a logical/rational plane.

Whether they realized it or not, it was that disconnect that Skipper and Jess were reacting to when they filled out the F-MOS. They knew that there was an animating spirit that had propelled those actions. They knew that those silly, goofy actions had come from a deep sense of love and caring.

So when all was said and done, it turns out that Matt and Jen had done a good job at attending to the Intangibles. In spite of – not because of – what they had done. Whether they realized it or not.

PART TWO

Getting a Firmer Grip
on the Solution

CHAPTER 7

A Widely Held – and False – Distinction

A FEW YEARS AGO, I was asked to develop a one-hour Intangibles module that was to be added to a company's three-day training program for new leaders – those who either had just been promoted into positions that would have them managing people for the first time in their careers or who would soon be assuming such first-time formal leadership responsibilities. To get a good sense of the context within which the to-be-developed Intangibles module would be used, I sat in on the delivery of the program in its then-current state as an observer.

The guest speaker near the end of the program's third and final day was Jeff, an executive who had just completed a two-year tour of duty as the aide-de-camp to Wayne, the company's CEO. Jeff's presentation was excellent. He was able to take many of the theories and principles that had been covered during the program and show how they had real-world application at the highest levels of the company. Judging by the attention level being paid by the attendees, you might even say that they were fully engaged.*

---

* See Scenario 2 on page 27–28.

Toward the end of his session, Jeff posed the following question: "What percentage of Wayne's time would you estimate he devotes to 'people stuff'?"

The answers were clustered in the 15–20 percent range. Jeff nodded, assuring all that their guesses were perfectly reasonable before hitting them with his punchline: "On a typical day, Wayne spends 50–60 percent of his time on people matters. That leaves him with just 40–50 percent of his time to focus on the business." At this, the thirty or so new leaders raised their eyebrows, shook their heads ruefully, and exchanged significant glances while dutifully scribbling notes in their program binders.

After offering a few closing remarks, Jeff gave a humbly grateful wave as he exited the room to enthusiastic applause. I was seated at the back of the room near the exit, so as Jeff passed me, I quietly arose and walked out of the room with him.

"Got a second?" I asked.

"Sure," Jeff replied.

I had gotten to know Jeff reasonably well from some previous work I had done with him, so I felt safe in offering a well-intentioned critique.

"That was terrific," I began, honestly. "But you said something toward the end that could have had the effect of undermining your message."

"Oh, dear," he said, genuinely concerned. "What was that?"

"You said that because Wayne spent 50–60 percent of his time on people stuff, he could only spend about 40–50 percent of his time 'on the business.'"

Although he was too polite to say so, Jeff's expression said it for him: "Yeah? So?"

"By phrasing it that way, you implied that time spent on the people stuff is not time spent 'on the business,'" I replied.

He gave a puzzled wince. I attempted an explanation.

"You just spent the better part of an hour making a compelling case for the importance of the people side of the leader's job, and the way you did it was spot on. But by wording things the way you did at the end, you put the people part of things over here [I gestured to my left] and 'running the business' over here [I gestured to my right]."

The light went on for Jeff. "*Now* I see what you're getting at," he said.

I felt relieved. I shouldn't have.

"I see it, but I don't agree with it," he continued. "I think you're splitting hairs, John. *They* got the message." And as he said this, he pointed back over his shoulder to the classroom from which we had just emerged. Then he looked at his watch: "I've really gotta run. Maybe we can pick this up later?"

"Sure, sounds good," I said, secure in the knowledge that this follow-up conversation would never happen.

In the years that have passed since this scenario unfolded, I've become more convinced than ever that my critique of Jeff's presentation did not represent hair-splitting at all. As a matter of fact, I'd go so far as to say that the disconnect that I had experienced with Jeff is right at the heart of everything discussed in these pages.

If we operate from the assumption that "the people stuff" is over here and "the business" is over there:

* We might recognize that being good at the people side of things is crucial to business success.

* We might take it seriously by, for example, inviting the CEO's former aide-de-camp to speak to a group of newly minted leaders about the importance of that people stuff.

* We might regularly survey employees about the people stuff, diligently examine the results, and put into place serious, substantial efforts designed to improve our performance along this or that people-related dimension on which we had come up short.

* We might, when the hoped-for improvements don't occur, redouble our efforts with even more serious, more substantial, and more best-practices-focused efforts.

But if things still don't measure up even after all of those redoubled efforts, we have left ourselves with a handy escape hatch: "I've really gotta run. Maybe we can pick this up later?"

Here's another way to look at things:

+ We do indeed have a business to run.

+ One hundred percent of what happens in the running of that business flows from what's done (or not done) by people. The business *is*, therefore, the sum total of the actions taken (or not taken) by those people.

+ The effectiveness of those actions depends on the degree to which those people are engaged, that is, the extent to which they bring the full measure of their skills, wisdom, and experience to the tasks at hand.

+ Engagement is fundamentally and profoundly affected by a leader's skill/facility/acumen at attending to the people stuff, a.k.a., the Intangibles.

+ Given all of the above, separating "the people stuff" from "running the business" represents a false distinction.

+ *Disabusing ourselves of that false distinction is step 1 along the path to getting a firmer handle on Engagement and the rest of those elusive Intangibles.*

Why is taking this first step so critical? Because it welds the escape hatch shut. It prevents us from adopting that all-too-familiar pose – palms up, shoulders shrugged, head cocked thirty degrees to the side, eyebrows raised, lips pursed tightly in regret – before invoking that all-purpose exculpatory mantra: "It's the people stuff. Whatayagonnado?"

There are historical precedents that demonstrate how welding shut such escape hatches can lead to dramatically improved business results.

Historical Precedent #1: Total Quality Management (TQM)

In the 1980s and early part of the '90s, Total Quality Management – TQM – was all the rage. This didn't happen because of leaders' sudden desire to achieve a platonic level of goodness in their business dealings. It happened because their companies were getting waxed competitively. Over time, dramatic and sometimes breathtaking progress was made in the application of the principles of TQM. But before that could happen, some long-standing assumptions had to be challenged.

Pre-TQM, the abiding mind-set was this: "Of course quality is a worthy goal, but people are imperfect, and entropy exists. So some number of defects will inevitably occur." Or said another way: "Whattayagonnado?"

Operating from this mind-set, businesses put in place a number of things to help mitigate that inevitability:

- ◆ There were quality departments, staffed by white-coated professionals armed with meters and calipers and clipboards.

- ◆ There were incoming inspection processes designed to weed out bad components and materials before they polluted the production line.

- ◆ As products became ever-more complex, there emerged ever-more sophisticated pieces of test equipment to help identify those inevitable defects.

- ◆ To salvage the value inherent in assemblies and sub-assemblies that had failed in-process inspections, there were repair and rework loops.

- ◆ There were even explicit declarations of Acceptable Quality Levels (AQLs), the precise-to-n-significant-digits level of defects that would be tolerated.

All of those quality departments and calipers and pieces of test equipment and rework loops and AQLs carried with them not inconsiderable dollar costs. But – Whattayagonnado? – defects are inevitable. And besides which, that's the way we'd always done things, we'd been successful at it in the past, so there was no compelling need to change.

Then Japan happened. Or more precisely, Japanese businesses began diligently applying the teachings of two Americans, W. Edwards Deming and Joseph M. Juran – the Ruth and Gehrig, respectively, of the quality movement. What had been a mark of poor quality, a label reading "Made in Japan," became the new gold standard as breakthrough improvements were made.

Essential to such breakthrough results was the adoption of three principles that challenged the abiding conventional wisdom:

1. A goal of a sound quality strategy must be to prevent defects from occurring in the first place as opposed to inspecting to identify defects after they have already occurred.

2. In the limit, the goal should be zero defects.

3. The fundamental unit of analysis should not be defects; rather, it should be the process that yielded such defects.

If ever the expression "prophets without honor in their native land" were a fitting one, it applies to Dr. Deming and Dr. Juran. There was nothing in what they taught Japanese industry that had not already been available, literally for decades, to American and other Western businesses.

Unfortunately, the abiding mind-set in the West said: "Sure, that stuff might work in Japan. But things are different over there. And besides which, things are going along pretty swimmingly with the way we've been handling quality around here, so we'll take a pass."

Here's the thing: the very existence of the things that represented "the way we do quality" were the cause of our inability to understand the existential threat posed by the new conventional wisdom as espoused by Deming and Juran.* All of those clipboards and calipers and AQLs and repair-and-rework loops had the effect

---

* And, to be sure, others.

of blocking our line of sight to a much better and far more profitable way of doing things. The cacophony created by all of that misguided activity drowned out the wisdom contained in the teachings of the good doctors.

At the root of it all? A presumptive "Whattaygonnado?" attitude.

Historical Precedent #2: Just-In-Time Inventory (JIT)

Even with our newfound wisdom vis-à-vis quality, we were in a transition period. We may have adopted prevention as our fundamental quality strategy as opposed to inspection. Philosophically speaking, we may have accepted that a goal of zero defects was do-able. And we may have begun focusing far more of our attention on the process that caused the defect rather than on the defect itself.

But until we reached that desired level of performance, some defects would still be occurring, some rework loops would still be necessary, and some mitigating strategies would still need to be in place.

One of those mitigating strategies was the carrying of additional inventories of raw materials, parts, sub-assemblies, assemblies, and even finished products to offset those still-inevitable defects. And even if there were no quality issues to contend with, surely economies of scale and the discounts associated with volume purchases would argue in favor of the need for carrying non-trivial inventories of parts and raw materials, wouldn't they?

As it happens, no, they wouldn't.

For one thing, all of that inventory carries with it substantial costs: the cost of the inventory itself, the cost of the physical plant needed to store that inventory, the cost to insure those assets, the cost of the people needed to manage and process and handle them, etc. At the risk of stating the obvious, added costs corrode competitive position.

Not only that, but the existence of that excess inventory and the systems to support it added a substantial inertial load to business operations. If one assumed steady state conditions, this was less of an issue. But as markets became more and more dynamic, that assumption became less valid, and that inertial load made it more difficult to manifest the kind of nimble and agile performance necessary to be competitive in those ever-faster-moving markets.

Enter Just-In-Time inventory – JIT – the first principle of which is this: Businesses should carry no inventory other than just the amount needed, where it's needed, when it's needed.

This posed what seemed to be a dilemma for even those practitioners who might be open to considering the adoption of JIT practices: "While I can see the validity of such an approach in theory, it can only work in practice if we have utter reliability in the quality of the parts and materials that are being delivered where and when they're needed, whether they're coming from upstream in our own production process or from external suppliers. Since we're not yet at that point, how can we reconcile theory with practice?"

That seems like a sensible and prudent response. As it turns out, though, there is no dilemma, and JIT principle number two explains why: Excess inventory does not insulate you from the effects of quality problems. Rather, it insulates those problems from their solutions.

A metaphor that's often invoked in discussions of JIT is that of "draining the swamp." While on the surface things may look placid and picturesque, at the bottom of the swamp are stumps and reeds and abandoned cars and other slimy unpleasantries. It's only after the swamp is drained that such slimy unpleasantries are revealed.

In the JIT metaphor, the excess inventory being carried is represented by the water. By eliminating excess inventory – that is, by "draining the swamp" – many more causes of quality problems are revealed than had previously been visible, and we are shaken out of the false sense of security that we were lulled into by that placid, picturesque surface view of things.

Eventually, dramatic progress was made as more and more businesses applied the principles of JIT. As with TQM, such progress would never have happened without a willingness to not be limited by long and deeply held assumptions.

In both cases, the systems and practices put into place based on those assumptions had the effect of blocking our line of sight to deeper solutions, and the cacophony created from those systems and practices had the effect of drowning out the wisdom of those who had already seen the light.

Historical Precedent #3: Lean

Over time, the insights at the heart of JIT led to what we now refer to as Lean, in which the bar has been further raised, from the elimination of excess inventory to the removal of all excess process steps – that is, steps that don't "add value."

After such dramatic progress made on the factory floor represented sufficient proof of concept, analogous steps were taken and breakthroughs realized in office and administrative processes and then on out to direct interaction with customers.

It wasn't just an accident of fate that these advances had their genesis in the eminently practical and tangible world of manufacturing. A broken or out-of-spec widget is something that can be seen and touched and measured. The dollar costs associated with all of that plant and equipment and inventory are large and obvious, and they translate boldly and directly to the bottom line.

But while the effects of less-than-ideal performance may be less direct in office or customer-facing environments, even administrative processes can be mapped. And there's nothing in the least abstract about an angry customer at the other end of a telephone line or pulled off onto the shoulder of a highway awaiting assistance.

Making the translation to the Intangibles, though, remains a major challenge since, by definition, they cannot be seen or touched or directly measured. That will be the topic of our next chapter.

By way of setting the stage for that discussion, herewith are a few questions for your consideration:

- What is an employee satisfaction survey if not an inspection?
- What are low survey scores related to the Intangibles if not defects?
- What is our presumptive willingness to devote extra time on

efforts designed to mitigate low employee survey scores if not what might be thought of as maintaining a safety stock of "time inventory"?

- How sure are we that all of the steps we go through in such mitigation efforts are, net, adding value?

- Could all of the programs and processes we're implementing in order to improve our results vis-à-vis the Intangibles actually be blocking our line of sight to the real issues? And drowning out the voices of those attempting to call our attention to those real issues?

- And, finally, what will we find if *that* swamp is drained?

CHAPTER 8

Draining the Swamp – Respect, Solipsism, and Employee Engagement

B EFORE ANSWERING THE QUESTION I posed at the end of the last chapter – What will we find if *that* swamp is drained? – there's a related question that needs to be considered: Why is the water so deep? What is it that's shielding our view of the problem that's at the root of our inability to achieve higher degrees of true Employee Engagement?

Quite a few things, actually:

* The research reports and conferences and articles purporting to identify "best practices" when it comes to attending more effectively to the Intangibles

* The processes and protocols and procedures that we've put into place as part of past well-intentioned efforts to implement those best practices

* The PowerPoint presentations we've generated and metrics we've tracked and rewards and recognition systems we've instituted to nudge people toward the kinds of behaviors that we understand to correlate to those best practices

- *And above all, the imprecision and inconsistency in the under-standing and usage of words and terms associated with Employee Engagement and other key Intangibles*

If I'm going to be perfectly honest about things, I have to concede that this book may well have poured a few more liters of water into the swamp:

- For one thing – and to invoke a highly technical term – this book contains a lot of stuff.

- Moreover, the effectiveness of all this stuff is limited by my ability to express what it all means in writing.

- As I wrote on page 14, there is inevitably going to be some loss of precision and clarity when using mere words to capture the essential characteristics of the Intangibles, since words are the only tools we have at our disposal to make a rational case about something that exists on a plane that is orthogonal to things rational.

- The story about the Wilsons represents an argument by analogy, which, by definition, is anything but a direct approach.

To mix the swamp metaphor with the metaphor introduced on page 12, the "water" that fills "the swamp" is all of those netted/euthanized/matted/framed butterflies that we've collected, when what we're really trying to get at is the gossamer essence of the thing.

Now that I've got you thoroughly confused with all of those swamps and butterfly nets and gossamer essences, let's try a thought experiment.

Suppose that Engagement and Empowerment and Trust and Value did not exist. Or to be a bit more precise, let's stipulate that while those Intangibles do exist, we haven't yet recognized them as rising to the level of concepts that we've decided to label and discuss and do something about.

Now suppose that the only Intangible that we have so-identified and labeled is Respect, properly understood. For simplicity's sake, let's introduce a convention to be used throughout the rest of this book. For our purposes, R! – the letter *R* with an exclamation point – will signify Respect, properly understood to mean *giving due consideration to the other.*

Why single out R!? Because it differs in kind from the others. It's the only one over which all of us have full control. No permission is needed before you can give due consideration to the other. No company-wide initiatives are necessary for you to manifest R!. No incremental resources are required. Rather, it's entirely up to the individual – at any time, on any day – as to whether or not he or she will infuse R! into whatever circumstances are at hand.

Unlike R!, the other Intangibles we've discussed are not directly within an individual's control. Rather, they're the result of other things having been done well:

- ◆ It's great to have people offering the full measure of their effort and energy to the tasks at hand – be Engaged.

- ◆ And it's great to have people feel safe while exercising judgment on the job – be Empowered.

- ◆ And it's great to have people manifest confident expectation when interacting with co-workers – be informed by a sense of Trust.

- ◆ And it's great to have little or no gap between our aspirational goals as a company and the degree to which we are living up to those goals – have our Values in practice be consonant with our Values as stated.

Whether or not any of those things happen, though, depends upon many, many factors that are well beyond any individual's immediate control. They are outputs, not inputs. They are destinations to be reached, not the fuel that will get you there.

R! is an input. R! is that fuel.

* * *

How might having a clear line of sight to R! make things better? Consider the case of the corporate vice president on page 25. As you'll recall, she was

> preparing for an offsite meeting for the top 150 leaders in her company, and she had asked me to look over a copy of the draft agenda and provide some feedback.
>
> The agenda items were pretty standard and straightforward: the just-closed quarter's business results, projections for the remainder of the fiscal year, updates on some key improvement projects, results of the latest employee opinion survey. Those sorts of things.
>
> "At first glance," I said to her, "these certainly seem like sensible enough things to be covering in a meeting like this." But then I pointed to some words that she had penciled in. "I notice that you've added *Small-Group Breakouts* here in the 2:00–3:00 time slot. What are people going to be doing during those breakouts?"
>
> "We haven't decided yet," she replied.
>
> Her answer caught me by surprise. "Then how do you know that breakouts are the best use of this hour?"
>
> Now it was her turn to be surprised. "We always have a breakout module in these meetings. We have to get people *engaged*." And when she said this, her tone suggested a sort of What-truck-did-this-guy-just-fall-off-of bewilderment.

But suppose that instead of being guided by a need to "get people engaged," she had been guided by a need to ensure that the agenda was viewed as a way of infusing maximum R! into the proceedings. Had that been the case, her penciled-in notation to the agenda might have been more like this:

> Who are the people attending the meeting? What's important to them? What's most likely to resonate with them?

Bear in mind that R! means giving "due" consideration to the other. The VP had some solid business objectives for the meeting, so it wasn't a matter of making sure that the agenda was sufficiently entertaining for the attendees. Had that been the case, she could have just hired some singers and dancers, some acrobats and jugglers, and been done with it. With R! as the informing notion, though, her thought process would have been more along these lines:

> *I've got these three objectives for the meeting. Given the meeting's attendee list – who they are, what's important to them, what will resonate with them – how should the meeting be structured to ensure that it yields the results that I'm after?*

Is that an easy question to answer? Not at all. But a necessary condition for coming up with a serviceable answer to a difficult question is that the question be asked in the first place.

Why, in our thought experiment, would the corporate VP have been more likely to ask just that question framed just that way? Because she would not have been distracted by the concept of Engagement, since, after all, no such concept had yet been identified and labeled.

With no easy out available to her – "We always have a breakout module in these meetings. We have to get people *engaged*." – she would have been left with no alternative other than a healthy infusion of R!, which in turn would have led to a better business outcome for her.

* * *

Now let's consider the senior leadership team described on page 43, as they

> listened intently as the vice president of human re-
> sources reported on the findings from a survey de-
> signed to measure Empowerment levels throughout
> the company.
>
> The results were disappointing, and the team's
> concern was obvious. The business unit's presi-
> dent seemed most concerned of all. He was usu-
> ally a stickler for staying on-agenda, but when the
> fifteen minutes that had been allotted for this dis-
> cussion had come to an end, he said: "I know our
> time's up, but this is important. Let's keep at it."
>
> Thirty minutes later, the president finally called
> time out. His reluctance was obvious when he said,
> "We've got to move on to other things." He turned
> to his vice president of quality: "It's clear that we've
> got some process problems that are causing people to
> think they're disempowered. Get your best Six Sigma
> people on it. Have them identify those process prob-
> lems and pull together teams to fix them."
>
> Then he turned his attention to his full team: "Let
> me be as clear as I can be. You are all empowered. I
> need you to go back to your people and make sure
> they know that *they* are empowered, *too!*"
>
> For just an instant, the vice president of market-
> ing looked like he wanted to say something. Just as
> quickly, though, he decided not to. When the meeting
> adjourned, I managed to get a private moment with
> him: "You looked like you were about to speak up."
>
> He nodded.
>
> "What was it you wanted to say?"
>
> "I wanted to say that we can tell our people they're

empowered until we're blue in the face, but if people don't feel empowered, then they're not empowered."

"Why didn't you say it?"

He furrowed his brow and shook his head. "Nope," he said. "Too risky."

The business's president was a good man, trying to do what he genuinely thought was best for the organization.

Let's consider all of the ways that his approach to the situation at hand represented the logical and sensible things to do:

+ In his mind, he had identified a clear problem statement: People don't realize that they're fully empowered.

+ The results of the latest survey could not have been more clear on this point, so he was being driven by facts and data, not by gut feeling.

+ He knew that in the vast majority of cases, when there was a problem at hand, it wasn't the fault of people for not doing things right. Rather, it was better to identify the process shortcomings that were causing well-meaning, dedicated people to serve up the undesirable results in question.

+ He had people on his staff who were highly trained in this sort of process analysis and intervention: a crack team of Six Sigma experts.

+ He gave his vice president of quality, in whose reporting chain resided all of those experts, clear and explicit direction.

+ And he knew that with any such problem, clear communication was essential. So after giving that charge to the quality VP, he issued an equally clear directive to the rest of his leadership team.

All of this was, indeed, highly logical and rational. But Empowerment is an Intangible – a feeling of safety while exercising judgment on the job – that resides on a different plane, one that's orthogonal to the logical/rational plane on which business people like to remain squarely grounded.

The president's past learning – logical, rational learning – about facts and data and best practices and process focus and communications had the effect of blocking his line of sight to the real problem at hand.

All of these things represented the sensible, best-practice-certified approach. As an added bonus, it enabled him to bask in the illusion of rigor provided by his comfort zone: "We've got an important problem. I have laid out a clear, sensible course of action. Who could take issue with it?"

As it happens, the vice president of marketing could have. But he chose not to. Why not? Because he knew that saying what was on his mind would be like shouting a warning to someone upwind in a hurricane. He wouldn't be heard, and he might get hit by deadly airborne debris in the process.

Let's now revisit the situation faced by the business unit's president, but this time we'll apply the rules of our thought experiment, where the concept of Empowerment had not yet been identified and labeled, where the only Intangible he had to work with was R!. Under that set of circumstances, his charge to his leadership team might have been more along these lines:

> People keep going to their bosses or directly to you – in some cases even to me – when they have difficult situations to deal with. They're always looking for direction – even permission – to do things that they're fully capable of doing on their own.
>
> This is an inefficient way to run the business. Not only is it more costly for us to be spending our time on things that can be handled by people at lower pay grades, it also slows things down and keeps us from being as fast and nimble as we need to be.

At this point he might have projected a PowerPoint slide that contained this sentence:

All of us have the responsibility to infuse the organization
with R! every chance we get.

Then he might turn back to his team and continue:

> You and I may know that our people are capable of
> doing the work without our direction or permission.
> If they weren't, they wouldn't be in the jobs they're in.
> But this isn't about what we know, it's about what they
> – the others – think.
>
> You and I may know that we've taken steps to
> change things. But this isn't about what we've done.
> It's about how those others have reacted to those
> things we've done.
>
> This is tricky stuff – a lot trickier than trying to
> identify the process step that's causing our widgets to
> be defective.

He might then raise his eyebrows, shrug, and hold out his hands, palms-up, in a beseeching gesture while asking: "Anybody got any ideas on this?"

At which point the vice president of marketing might say: "There are times when I hold back, when I'm not sure I have the authority to make a call or to be as candid as I might be."

Here the president's eyebrows might go from raised to furrowed: "Why wouldn't you?"

"Because," might come the marketing VP's reply, "I didn't feel safe in doing so." At which point the cat, as it were, would have been belled.

How realistic is this R!-fueled scenario? I don't know. What I do know, though, is that it – or something like it – would be a whole lot more productive than the way the scenario had actually unfolded in the real world.

More to the point, it's a scenario that's a whole lot more likely to oc-cur if it's informed by a felt-need to sharpen the focus on the other; if it's fueled, that is, by the need to infuse R! throughout the organization at

117

every opportunity. And *that's* a whole lot more likely to occur if the line of sight leading to it isn't blocked by a misunderstanding of the concept of Empowerment and the easy out it can provide.

It could be argued, in fact, that things went off the rails as soon as the situation at hand was viewed as "a problem to be solved" as opposed to "a complex situation to be managed." That's because "a problem to be solved" is catnip to anyone whose thought processes skew to the logical/rational, and because the "situation at hand" exists on that other, orthogonal plane.

And that way, as we all know, be dragons.

* * *

Or consider the scenario described in Chapter 4a (Toward More Practical Definitions of *Trust* and *Respect*), the one about receiving the e-mail from your boss that read:

"*NOT what I was looking for!!!*"

Why might a leader send such an e-mail?

Let's dispose of the easy and obvious answer first: The leader in question is one of those very bad words that rhymes with brass pole. But since this book is not aimed at people for whom sociopathy is seen as a core competence, we'll move on.

For our purposes, it's more interesting – and more realistic – to ask: "Why would a leader who is a good and well-intentioned person send such an e-mail?"

The likeliest answer is that he or she had had a bad day, was highly stressed owing to all of the issues that were slopping over the edges of his or her already full plate, and had – to invoke another not terribly elegant term – screwed up.

It happens. All of us know this. And when it happens, we probably feel remorse for having done such a thing. We might even call the recipient of the e-mail into our office to make amends, which is the right and noble thing to do.

But what if we were able to offload some of the things that were raising the noise levels in our day-to-day dealings? More specifically, what if we could remove the talk-talk-talk and the meetings and the PowerPoint presentations and the survey results and the Lucite tchotchkes that have heretofore gone with our well-intentioned efforts to attend more effectively to the Intangibles, which we know to be important, but – dammit – we've got a business to run and people need to be a little more thick-skinned when we screw up like this, *don't they?!*

What if – as is the case in our thought experiment – the only Intangible that had been identified and labeled was R!. And what if we had a poster hanging on our office walls much like the PowerPoint slide that the business president projected in the Empowerment scenario above:

All of us have the responsibility to infuse the organization
with R! every chance we get.

Would we not be considerably less likely to write such an e-mail? Or at least to take a beat before clicking on SEND?

The power of a more single-minded focus on R! has to do with fostering an atmosphere of what we have come to label as Trust, which in turn will help people have a deeper feeling of what we have come to label as Empowerment, which in turn will result in people who are more deeply and fully characterized by what we have come to label as Engagement, *because all of the above will result in higher levels of efficiency, shorter cycle times, lower levels of employee turnover, and a substantially higher ROI to the owners of the business!*

This is about business results, not about being good guys or gals. If you happen to be in an industry where sociopathic behavior is seen as a requirement to producing those attractive ROIs, then have at it. If, on the other hand, you work in a somewhat more highly evolved environment, then establishing an ethos informed by R! might be the better way for you to go, since R! is the fundamental nutrient of organizational health.

* * *

Which brings us to R! and Values. I've already ranted at some length in Chapter 5a about the pitfalls and sensitivities inherent in talking explicitly about Values, so I'll make this quick by telling you the story of a large company that went to great lengths to ensure that employees were very much aware of the company's stated Values. Any flat surface not already covered by signage was a potential site for posters, display cases, or flat-screens broadcasting lists of, paeans to, or testimonials about those stated Values. Legend had it that a former high-ranking executive at one company facility would stop people in the halls to administer pop Values quizzes; things did not go well for anyone who failed the quiz.

One of the company's stated Values was "People," so an Employee Appreciation Day was held each year. A large tent was raised in one of the company's parking lots. Rows of tables and chairs were brought in, and lunch would be served by company executives to all employees.

Such a visible sign of the company valuing its people is a powerful thing. On a practical level, it's great to give people a free lunch, especially one that was much better than the usual cafeteria fare, as well as a more leisurely time slot than usual in which to enjoy it. On a more philosophical level, what better example of "servant leadership" could there be than the company's executive team donning aprons (and in the case of one brave vice president, a chef's toque), and, literally, serving the hoi polloi?

There was one problem, though. Someone eavesdropping on the table talk under the tent would have heard more than a few comments along the lines of this: "They think that giving us a free lunch makes up for treating us like drones the rest of the year." "Did you see the way VP A was ladling out the soup? It was pretty clear that he did *not* want to be here!" "At least he showed up! VP B saw this as an opportunity to delegate." (Side note: It was VP B who had actually sent the *"NOT what I was looking for!!!"* e-mail, so she at least gets points for consistency.)

When the gap between Values as stated and Values in practice is small or nonexistent, then such oh-so-public events can indeed be effective. When the gap is a large one, though, such events can actually do damage. They are the logical equivalent of taping a Kick Me! sign to your back. A little less focusing on What can we do? and a little more R! – What effect will it have on the other? – and you're more likely to avoid such missteps.

* * *

So if more frequent and abundant infusions of R! are what it takes to get this sort of progress, and if R! means *giving due consideration to the other*, then after the swamp has been drained, what we would find is our tendency to not give such sufficient consideration to the other. There is a word for this tendency, and that word is *solipsism*:

A theory in philosophy that your own existence is the only thing that is real or can be known

Granted, *solipsism* is a pretty obscure word. Why use it when there are other, more familiar words such as *self-absorption* or *self-centeredness* readily available? Precisely *because* it's obscure.

One theme of this book has been the price we pay in our ability to attend more effectively to the Intangibles because of inconsistent and/or imprecise usage of seemingly familiar words, such as *Trust* and *Empowerment* and *Engagement* and, especially, *Respect*. With *solipsism*, we start with a clean slate. We don't have to unlearn the definitions we've been using in the past. As a result, its obscureness becomes a feature, not a bug.

All of which leads me to an assertion:

Solipsism – both institutional and individual – is the root cause of our inability to attend more effectively to the Intangibles.

Institutional solipsism is the tacit assumption that all that matters is what goes on here at the company. What happens outside these walls is irrelevant. To the extent that such external considerations are thought about at all, they are seen as distractions or sources of annoyance.

121

One marker of institutional solipsism is the term *work/life balance.* Think about what that term says: There's what you do at work, and then there's your life. But that's not how employees – all of those "others" who don't so much as exist in an institutionally solipsistic worldview – see things. Their perspective is more likely along these lines: "My job is a part of my life. It's a very important part, but I'm a fully formed adult with family responsibilities, and my work in my community, and my hobbies, etc., etc., etc."

The boss who sent the *"NOT what I was looking for!!!"* e-mail back in Chapter 4a was likely operating from a pretty solipsistic point of view: "I'm very busy! I don't always have the time to be diplomatic!"

Please note that the invocation of solipsism is meant as a diagnosis, not as an indictment. Entropy being what it is, a tendency toward solipsism is the natural state of things. Where can the countervailing force come from? From constant infusions of R! – from adopting the discipline to always give due consideration to the other.

Said another way, solipsism is the disease, R! is the antidote.

R! begets Trust. Trust begets Empowerment. Empowerment begets Engagement. Engagement begets a greater return on your investment in human capital. A greater return on your investment in human capital begets a better financial ROI for your shareholders.

Isn't that the way it's supposed to work? Isn't that the point of the exercise? Of trying to get better at the people stuff, at attending more effectively to the Intangibles?

CHAPTER 9

On Being More "Other-Wise"

INTRODUCED TWO NOTIONS in the last chapter:

1. Solipsism: a theory in philosophy that your own existence is the only thing that is real or can be known, and the root cause of our difficulty in being able to attend more effectively to the Intangibles

2. R!: Respect, properly defined as *giving due consideration to the other* and the antidote to solipsism

To this point, the discussion of just what *due consideration to the other* might mean has focused on the effects of what one says (or doesn't say) and does (or doesn't do) on the other. For example:

* The person in Chapter 4a who received the *"NOT what I was looking for!!!!"* e-mail

* The vice president of marketing in Chapter 3a who thought that it was too risky to speak up about the way the business unit's president was approaching Empowerment

* The people in Chapter 2a who were participating in a pointless breakout session and regretted having accepted the meeting invitation in the first place

There is no question that *due consideration to the other* speaks to such examples and that it's important to consider the effect one is having on the other. But this raises a key question:

How can you know – in advance –
what those effects might be?

Well, if being effective as a leader means having a high degree of Employee Engagement, and if the degree of Engagement is a function of R!, and if the degree of R! depends on the extent to which you give due consideration to the other, then doesn't it stand to reason that you will have a better sense of what those effects might be if you know who the other is – what matters to him or her, what makes him or her tick, what will resonate with him or her? And, most important of all, could it be that owing to a high degree of institutional solipsism, you might not be giving due consideration to the potential *positive* effect that the other might have on the business, that he or she might have some life experience that falls outside the bounds of your job descriptions and process maps that could add substantial value to your efforts, that they might even have had a good idea or two that was developed while working in a building that did not have your company's logo on the door?

Consider a hypothetical. Suppose all of a leader's followers are exactly like the leader in every way. They think the same way. Their learning style is the same. Their likes and dislikes are the same. Their strengths and weaknesses are the same. And so on and so forth.

How well would such a leader "know" her followers? Pretty well. In this case, giving due consideration to the other would probably boil down to making sure that their names were spelled correctly on their paychecks.

Now let's consider a far less hypothetical example – the president of a corporation presiding over a leadership team meeting in the 1960s. How well did he (and it would have been a he) know the members of that leadership team? Quite well. They were pretty much all fifty-ish-year-old, white, Anglo-Saxon Protestant males.

But that's no longer the world in which we live. Now the *due* in *due consideration* brings with it many more factors, such as age co-hort, gender, sexual orientation, ethnicity, degree of able-ness, etc.

Does being attentive to such demographic categories represent a higher order of due consideration? It can. But it can also represent a kind of enlightenment on the cheap. Why on the cheap? Because those categories are objective and measurable. They represent a way of doing something about the people stuff without having to stretch any conceptual muscles since it fits our rational/tangible bias.*

Consider two followers on an org chart:

- Jim is a twenty-eight-year-old, epileptic, bi-sexual male of Armenian ancestry.

- Gladys is a sixty-one-year-old mother of three and grand-mother of six whose parents immigrated to the United States from Ireland, who has been married to her high school sweetheart for forty-two years, who attends daily Mass, and whose sexual orientation we do not know because, as she puts it, "It's none of your g**d*** business!"

Do we now know some useful and important things about Jim and Gladys? Yes, we do.

Do we know enough to know just what the *due* in *due consideration* means for each of them? No. Or at least not unless we're going to make judgments based on stereotypes.

Which brings us right to angst-provoking ground zero of the Intangibles. Because we know that we need to know what makes people tick. We know that it's important. We know that it's what makes effective leaders effective. And we know that it's bloody hard to do.

Human nature being what it is, easy is more attractive than hard. If there's an easy way out – an escape hatch – we'll use it, by equating diversity with demographics, by commissioning the construction of eight-foot-high, three-dimensional letters spelling R-E-S-P-E-C-T to line the entry road to the employee parking lot, by making videos that

---

* This is why some people have philosophical concerns about the extent to which formal diversity efforts focus on demographics. They get a jolt of cognitive dissonance caused by an instinctive sense that something deeper is being missed.

equate Respect with a handshake and a "Hi, nice to meet you."

We use those escape hatches to avoid having to actually come to grips with the true nature of the challenge at hand – if, that is, it were possible to grip something that's Intangible.

Even as we crawl through those escape hatches, though, there's a part of us – what Lincoln described as "the better angels of our nature" – that, deep down, knows that we're avoiding something important, that we're copping out.

That's where that angst comes from.

* * *

The only reason that being effective at attending to the Intangibles is important is that it will lead to better business results. Said another way, the reason the soft stuff matters is that it has a big effect on the hard stuff.

Now, it's an economic truism that "most interesting things happen at the margin." Other things being equal, whoever is able to offer an additional increment of value to the customer – a bit of added value *at the margin* – will win out.

In the '80s and '90s, that marginal advantage redounded to companies that were the earliest to get religion about TQM. A decade or so later, that edge went to those who diligently and effectively applied the principles of JIT. Still later, those who applied the principles of Lean to a fuller range of business processes – including those outside of the factory – gained the competitive edge.

By now, though, pretty much everybody knows and has applied those principles. (Those who haven't have been left behind, if they're still in business at all.) The reason there has been so much attention paid in recent years to things such as Engagement is that we have come to sense – not quite "know," but "sense" – that Engagement is where the source of competitive advantage now resides. We've done the value-added flow analyses and process-improvement projects – the hard, tangible stuff – and we've reached the point of diminishing returns. We kinda/sorta know that – are afraid that? – the marginal edge is now going to have to come from the soft stuff, from being better at attending to Engagement and other key Intangibles.

Dealing with the Intangibles has always caused a fair amount of discomfort. Knowing that such uncomfortable subject matter will now be the terrain on which competitive battles must be fought won't help.

Higher levels of Employee Engagement *should be* your objective; the research is clear and compelling on that point. Tapping into higher levels of effort, energy, and expertise that your employees have to offer *will* increase the return on your investment in human capital.

Will this be easy to do? Hell no. But remember: you don't have to be perfect at it. You just have to be better. Better than you were yesterday and better – at the margin – than the competition.

* * *

In a very broad sense, this book was written in a very linear way:

- My first thought was: Otherwise Engaged *would make a great title.*

- My next thought was: *Now all I have to do is write a book to go with it.*

The reason that I was so taken with *Otherwise Engaged* as a title is that I thought it made a nice double-pun:

- *Otherwise Engaged*, as in: *If you want to be more effective at attending to the Intangibles, you need to take an approach to the whole notion of Engagement other than the one you've been taking.*

And:

- *Otherwise Engaged*, as in: *If you want to be more effective at attending to the Intangibles, you need to develop a laser-like focus on the other.*

After completing the first draft, I went down this line of thinking:

* *The book makes sort of a big deal about the notion of* the other. (Perhaps you've noticed.)

* *Is there a way for the title to do a bit more work without losing the two halves of the pun?*

I thought about revisiting an idea that I had discarded some time earlier and introducing the concept of *Othership*, which could be defined as: *maintaining a laser-like focus on and deep awareness of* the other. *Othership* could then take its place in the lexicon alongside *Leadership* and *Followership*.

But I was afraid that *Othership* might be a bit too precious. Plus which, we'd probably all be better off with fewer rather than more neologisms in our lexicons. So I began brainstorming phrases containing *the other: Focused on the Other, Attuned to the Other, In Synch with the Other, Aware of the Other, Smarter About the Other, Knowledgeable about the Other, Wiser about the Other.*

That's it! Wiser about the Other! *Other-Wise*, which morphed into *OtherWise*, which, I thought, preserved both halves of the pun while coining a term that puts the focus right where it belongs: on the need to become more other-wise if we're going to survive, much less thrive, in the years to come.

The more I thought of it, though, I became convinced that changing the title to *OtherWise Engaged* or *Other-Wise Engaged* might also be a bit too precious, not to mention heavy-handed. So I went back to the original title, *Otherwise Engaged*. But if one of the other versions – *Other-Wise* or *OtherWise* – serves as a useful heuristic, then by all means have at it. No extra charge.

CHAPTER 10

Conclusion – A (Perhaps Not So) Modest Proposal

"Simplify, simplify."
— *Henry David Thoreau*

"One 'simplify' would have sufficed."
— *Ralph Waldo Emerson*

For decades, businesses dealt with quality issues in the traditional ways that, at the time, represented best practices. Lots of inspection. Lots of rework loops. Lots of additional inventory of parts and materials to make up for the inevitable losses in scrap and rework following all of those inspections. Then somebody said: "All of those things that you're doing to solve your quality problems are actually *causing* those problems. They're blocking your line of sight to the real root causes, which reside in your work processes." And enormous progress was made.

For decades, businesses dealt with inventory issues in the traditional ways that, at the time, represented best practices. Stock up to take advantage of volume discounts. Keep enough on hand to supply planned production as well as rework owing to quality issues. Invest in the people and physical plant needed to store and manage that inventory in the best, most efficient ways possible. Then somebody said: "Your interpretation of the problem at hand is blocking your line of sight to its real solution. All of that inventory is preventing you from realizing the kinds of efficiency and agility to be gained by adopting a just-in-time approach to inventory management." And enormous progress was made.

For decades, businesses have understood the need to attend more effectively to the Intangibles. More recently, the focus has been on the concept of Engagement and the substantial increases in business performance that go with it. Well-intentioned, well-funded efforts have been made and conferences have been held and studies have been done, all of which have had the effect of describing a collection of best practices.

What I am perhaps not so modestly proposing is that all of those efforts and conferences and studies and best practices are blocking our line of sight to the root of the problem, that that problem is a tendency toward institutional and individual solipsism, and that the antidote to solipsism is Respect, properly understood to mean *giving due consideration to the other*, where that "other" is not a cipher or a face on an employee ID badge, but a living, breathing human being, and where R! – Respect, properly understood – is the fundamental nutrient of organizational health.

Don't get me wrong. I'm not a Pollyanna. I most assuredly do *not* think that if we just showed each other a little more Respect we'd all be transported into a world of unicorns and comfy chairs. It isn't that easy.

But it is, in fact, that simple. And simple is hard, as suggested by Thoreau's famous quote and Emerson's wonderfully ironic reply that appear at the beginning of this chapter.

As a matter of fact, trying to make things simple poses something of a dilemma for me. For the past 130 pages, I've been arguing that we have to let go of some of the assumptions we've been making about the Intangibles – to embrace their "intangibleness," to stop thinking in terms of *What to do?* and first start coming to grips with *What effect will they have on the other?*

But unless I provide some specific prescriptive steps, this will all have been an exercise in abstract thinking, which can be nice but which also won't get you very far. Herewith, then, some prescriptive steps that are consistent with this book's central argument:

1. Stop talking about most of the Intangibles that have been covered in these pages.

   ◆ Stop talking about Trust. Instead, start creating an environment in which it becomes easier for the other to feel confidence in what can be expected from you.

   ◆ Stop talking about Empowerment. Instead, start creating an environment in which the other will feel safe while exercising judgment on the job.

   ◆ Stop talking about Engagement. Instead, start creating an environment in which others will be more likely to bring to bear the full measure of their effort and energy on the tasks at hand.

   ◆ Stop talking about Values. Instead, start creating an environment in which *what really matters around here* is in better alignment with your institutional aspirations.

2. If you must invoke those words, invoke them as adjectives instead of as nouns. Not *Engagement* but *Engaged*. Not *Empowerment* but *Empowered*. Why?

   ◆ A noun is a thing, an entity unto itself: We're over here, and it – the noun – is over there.

     ◆ "We need more Engagement. Let's order some up!"

     ◆ "When will the next shipment of Empowerment arrive?"

   ◆ An adjective can't exist by itself. It modifies something else. Saying "engaged" or "empowered" suggests the existence of something else.

   ◆ What is that something else? A person. An other.

- Which is precisely the point. Engagement or Empowerment are not things that we do/create. They're things that reside within *the other*.

- See the difference?

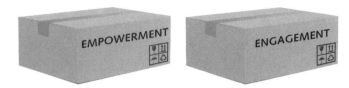

3. Start focusing all your efforts vis-à-vis the Intangibles on creating an ethos of R!.

  - Make sure everyone knows that Respect, properly understood, means giving due consideration to the other.

  - Introduce the concept of solipsism – both institutional and individual – and make sure others understand its corrosive effect on the culture you want to create.

  - Remember that the obscureness of the word *solipsism* is a feature, not a bug.

  - Although I'm not big on slogans and posters:

    - Take advantage of the fact that solipsism comes with its own built-in slogan that lends itself to a handy shorthand: "SOS – Stamp Out Solipsism."

    - If you must make posters, consider this one:

4. Metrics are also important, so here's the metric I'd recommend vis-à-vis R!: the percentage of people who pass "The Mirror Test" each day. Here's how to implement The Mirror Test:

    *   Next to the door/exit of each person's workspace, hang a mirror. Instruct everyone to, before leaving each day:

        *   Look into the mirror.

        *   Ask yourself this question: "In doing my job today, did I give due consideration to the other?"

        *   Record your answer.

        *   Submit it.

        *   Go home.

    *   That's it. Simple to implement. Hard as hell to pass.

* * *

In the "Introduction," I told my "Piano Man" story and said that it was one of two incidents that have most brightly illuminated the nature of the challenge at hand when it comes to attending more effectively to the Intangibles. Here's the other one.

My assignment had me working closely with Ned, a senior manager in the company's HR department who was responsible for leadership development programs. He had just completed a research project designed to identify those specific behaviors most closely associated with highly rated leadership performance.

The research methodology Ned employed was simple and straightforward:

*   Some 5,000 employees had been surveyed, approximately one-third of the company's entire workforce.

*   Included within those 5,000 survey subjects were suitable representations of all functions, all job grades, all demographic categories, and all geographic locations.

- Survey respondents were first asked to rate the leadership effectiveness of the person to whom they directly reported along a 5-point scale, with a rating of 5 meaning "Excellent" and 1 meaning "Poor."

- Respondents were then given a list of several dozen generally recognized leadership behaviors and asked: "To what extent does your leader demonstrate each of the following behaviors?" This was also done along a 5-point scale, with 5 meaning "Always" and 1 meaning "Never."*

Ned then explained to me how he had been able to identify the ten leadership behaviors most closely associated with the highest-rated leaders. He emphasized that while there has been no shortage of research done over the years for business in general, the fact that this survey had been done exclusively within his company added validity to the results he had gotten. I told him that I couldn't agree more.

But our thinking began to part ways when Ned said the following: "What we need to do now is to develop programs to help leaders get better at those ten behaviors. If we do that right, our leadership effectiveness results should improve."

"If you do that, you might see improved results," I replied, "but I wouldn't be so sure that you'd be getting at the root of the issue."

"What makes you say that?" Ned asked, with a puzzled look.

"I think you may be confusing correlation with causality,"† I said.

At this, Ned's expression changed from puzzlement to displeasure. Hoping to make amends, I added, "It's a very common mistake." That didn't help.

Undaunted, I soldiered on. "Your strategy is based on the assumption that if you can get leaders – people who manage other people – to manifest and improve those ten behaviors, they will then be better leaders."

---

* Behaviors to be rated included such things as upholding high ethical standards, demonstrating business acumen, setting priorities, delegating, listening, communicating, evaluating performance, resolving conflict, collaborating across functions, etc.
† For readers who enjoyed our earlier excursion into a dead language, here's the Latinate way of saying this: *Post hoc ergo propter hoc* (After which, therefore because of which).

Ned nodded, but it was clear that he was still not 100 percent pleased with the trajectory of our conversation.

I continued. "There's another hypothesis that ought to be tested. It could be that better leaders are the people who are simply more characterologically predisposed to do those ten things. It's that innate characteristic in someone who is a good leader that people sense, not the behaviors themselves."

Now Ned was clearly conflicted. "I hear what you're saying," he said. "But even if you're right, what can we do about it?"

"You can delve more deeply into the characteristics of those leaders who were highly rated," I replied.

"But you don't understand," Ned said. "I had a hard enough time getting company leadership to okay this research. If I go back to them now and say that we have to do more, they aren't going to buy it. This gives us hard data to support programs that can help lead to visible, observable behaviors, things that we can see and point to. What you're suggesting leaves us with nothing we can see, nothing that we can get our arms around."

Exactly so. That eighty-word answer from Ned represents the most succinct, clear-eyed, and heartfelt statement of the core problem at hand that I have ever heard.

Which brings us to a very old joke:

> A man is driving along a city street and comes to a corner. As he makes a right turn, he notices another man on his hands and knees on the sidewalk, under a street lamp.
>
> The driver stops the car, gets out, and approaches the other man.
>
> "Are you all right?" he asks.
>
> "Yes," answers the man on his hands and knees. "I'm fine. I'm just looking for my car keys."
>
> The first man says, "You're pretty sure this is where you lost them?"
>
> "Not really," says the man on his hands and knees. "But the light's better here."

Taking on the challenge of dealing more effectively in the domain of the Intangibles makes many (most?) leaders uncomfortable. While we understand that it's important, we just find it hard to get a solid grip on such things. And when you think about it, that makes perfect sense, since – by definition – you can't touch an Intangible.

What do we do? We do the things that have made us successful in the past, such as chartering teams, and mapping processes, and designing and implementing communications plans, and defining and tracking metrics, and measuring progress, and making mid-course corrections, and what not. And when we do that, we think that we're doing the best we can vis-à-vis the Intangibles. After all, when we look around, we see that that's what other people are doing, so how far off can we be?

Said another way, we look where the light is better. This is exactly what Ned's instincts were telling him about how to proceed based on the research he had done regarding leadership behaviors. Trouble is, that's not where the keys are.

One key lies in accepting and embracing the fact that the Intangibles are … intangible. As such, they are orthogonal to the rational/logical issues with which business people are more comfortable dealing.

Another lies in disabusing ourselves of the false distinction between "running the business" and "the people stuff" – that in the limit, all a business is is its people.

Still another key lies in coming to the humbling realization that pretty much everybody who makes up your business isn't you; they are all "the other."

Finally, embracing the fact that everything you say (or don't say) and do (or don't do) has the potential to affect those others.

So we face a choice.

We can put together teams, and research best practices, and perform analyses comparing our historical performance with those best practices and then create project and program plans to improve things vis-à-vis Engagement and Empowerment and company Values and Trust & Respect – we might even toss a few more into the stew, such as Diversity and Integrity – and integrate all of the individual project plans into an overarching master plan that captures in one view every jot and tittle of each of those individual plans, showing the relative progress of each, thereby enabling us to do a better job of monitoring progress and making any necessary mid-course corrections … all the while realizing that each of those efforts overlaps with all the others, suggesting the need for models and Venn diagrams making clear the relative importance and areas of overlap, thereby enabling us to make now-better-informed mid-course corrections … all the while making sure that we have the systems and metrics in place to recognize and reward people's efforts related to this important work … people, that is, who aren't all the same, calling for even more sophisticated processes and analyses and mechanisms to enable us to see all kinds of differences in demographic categories and subject matter expertise and life experience and educational and professional background … interjecting at the appropriate times the results of all-hands surveys … overlaying the results of said surveys onto what we've done to date so that we can make still better mid-course corrections and monitor and measure and improve and recognize and reward … and on and on it goes, at all times doing good, sensible, leadership stuff.

Or we can go down a simpler path, recognizing that the one thing that we can pretty much control is the extent to which people are treating each other with Respect, and asking ourselves at the end of each day: Did I give due consideration to the other?

We can become, as the title of this book suggests, Otherwise Engaged:

- ◆ Otherwise Engaged, as in adopting an approach to Engagement that is other than the one traditionally used

- ◆ Otherwise Engaged, as in ensuring that this approach has a laser-sharp focus on how what we do (and don't do) and say (and don't say) affects the other

Make no mistake. While that second path may be simpler, it is by far the more difficult one to traverse.

Because along that path, there are no PowerPoint slides or Venn diagrams or PERT charts to hide behind. No cacophonous din to distort meaningful signals into misleading noise. No colleagues to disappoint you by misunderstanding an order or missing a deadline.

There's just you, looking into a mirror, and considering your answer to a simple question – "Did I give due consideration to the other?" – knowing that the answer can only come from someplace within your heart and soul.

Which is as it should be, since that's where the Intangibles, properly understood, reside. That's where the keys can be found.

ACKNOWLEDGMENTS

THIS IS A BOOK about the importance of being attuned to "the other." That this is the single most important characteristic manifested by effective leaders is what makes this a business book.

Developing such "attuned-ness" is less a matter of registering for a class and more one of absorbing it while – to borrow Tom Peters' wonderful phrase – "wobbling toward clarity" in one's personal and professional lives.

When it comes to such deeply important subject matter, my parents, Harry and Antoinette, were my teachers and role models. My brother David learned well from them, and I continue to learn from him.

My wife Gail is the only person on the planet for whom being part of my family was optional. As these words are written, she has taken on the challenge of attempting to tune in to me for more than 37 years, and I thank her for that. That I have had the privilege of tuning in to her over that same time period has been, quite simply, a joy.

Raising children is a terrifyingly exhilarating experience, one that calls for a high degree of attuned-ness to the other. Our kids are now adults. Mike is 31 and Joanna is 28, and I am constantly impressed by their insightfulness about and charity toward others, wonderful characteristics that I can assure you came for far more from Gail than they did from me.

Ken Lizotte served as my agent and advisor on this project. Jim Pennypacker is the founder of Maven House Press, and has been my editor, publisher, and advisor throughout the process. Lucia and Gloria Cortina were the artistic talent behind the illustrations gracing these pages. My thanks to all of you.

I did a lot wobbling toward clarity while growing up in my home town, in college and graduate school, as an employee of a number of companies, and as a consultant to dozens more. The names listed below in alphabetical order are people to whom I owe much when it comes to my personal and professional development, and this is my far too small way of thanking them. Sadly, some are no longer with us, but that is not a good reason for failing to acknowledge them here. That I'm sure I've left some names off that should be here serves as proof that I still have much to learn when it comes to attuned-ness. So ... Meredith Allen, Bob Anderson, Fr. Maurice Amen, Joe Baldanza, Bill Band, Dave Berlew, Bill Blake, Bob Boculac, Joe Bonito, Matthew Budman, Dan Ciampa, Gale Connell, Tony Corvo, Steve Crom, Fr. John Culloty, Calvin Denning, John Doerr, Carolyn Drew, Chris Dunphy, Ralph Feola, John Ferrie, Bill Finch, Randy Gerdes, Tim Glaeser, Chris Gonsalves, Elmer Grapenstetter, Tracey Gray, Dave Hartman, Ed Hay, Dave Haines, Rob Held, Bill Kelly, Bob Kennedy, Dick Larkin, Steve Leduc, Ron Mallis, Larry McAuliffe, Stuart McComas, Greg Moffatt, Larry Moulter, Mike Murnane, Tom Mueller, Stacey Philpot, Frank Pompeii, Ed Rahaim, Paul Reese, Hank Rej, Peg Riley, Nort Salz, Lee Silvestre, Dan Smith, Jim Smith, Scott Sneath, Elisabeth Swan, Brian Wigton, Janice Young, and Hank Zolla ... thank you so much for all that you've taught and given me over the years.

INDEX

141

ABOUT THE AUTHOR

FOR THE PAST THIRTY YEARS, John Guaspari has helped leaders take on the challenge of being more effective at attending to the so-called Intangibles.

He is the author of six previous books on the topic, including the best-selling *I Know It When I See It*, *The Customer Connection*, and *The Value Effect*, seven best-selling training videos, as well hundreds of articles and columns. He has worked with corporate clients in scores of industries, and he has delivered some 1,500 intangibles-related presentations, seminars, and workshops, invariably receiving highest ratings from attendees and participants.

As a result, John has gained an enviable reputation for his ability to unravel complex subject matter and communicate it in the kind of accessible and engaging way that leads to real learning. Said another way, he knows how to be engaging about Engagement.

Long before entering the world of consulting, he began his professional career as an aerospace engineer and then went on to hold corporate positions in such widely varying functions as marketing, customer support, quality, leadership development, and organizational effectiveness.

He lives in North Attleboro, Massachusetts, with his wife Gail and her – not "their" but "her" – four cats. His hobbies include golf, obsessive reading, and avoiding water sports.